Pub Strolls in

CHESHIRE

James F. Edwards

COUNTRYSIDE BOOKS
NEWBURY BERKSHIRE

COUNTRYSIDE BOOKS
3 Catherine Road
Newbury, Berkshire

To view our complete range of books,
please visit us at
www.countrysidebooks.co.uk

ISBN 1 85306 659 1

*In memory of John Hubbert, a good man,
who loved the countryside and is
greatly missed by his family and friends.*

Photographs by the author
Maps by the author and redrawn by
Gelder design & mapping

Designed by Graham Whiteman

Produced through MRM Associates Ltd., Reading
Printed in Singapore

Contents

AREA MAP SHOWING LOCATION OF THE WALKS

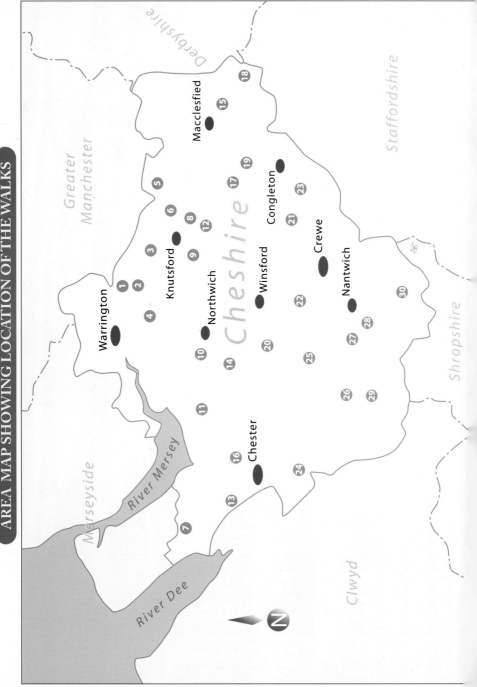

WALK

PUBLISHER'S NOTE

We hope that you obtain considerable enjoyment from this book; great care has been taken in its preparation. However, changes of landlord and actual closures are sadly not uncommon. Likewise, although at the time of publication all routes followed public rights of way or permitted paths, diversion orders can be made and permissions withdrawn.

We cannot, of course, be held responsible for such diversion orders and any inaccuracies in the text which result from these or any other changes to the routes nor any damage which might result from walkers trespassing on private property. We are anxious though that all details covering the walks and the pubs are kept up to date and would therefore welcome information from readers which would be relevant to future editions.

The sketch maps accompanying each walk are not always to scale and are intended to guide you to the starting point and give a simple but accurate idea of the route to be taken. For those who like the benefit of detailed maps, we recommend that you arm yourself with the relevant Ordnance Survey map in the Landranger series.

This book is for those who wish to undertake leisurely strolls through attractive scenery. Each route commences at an appealing inn and also provides an opportunity to visit places of interest, such as historic houses, parks and gardens, water mills, museums, potteries, towns, villages, garden centres, castles, workshops and well-known features in the landscape. The strolls are, geographically, evenly spread throughout the county – from Lymm in the north to Audlem in the south and from Willaston-in-Wirral in the west to Wildboarclough in the east. The length of the strolls average out at about 3 miles with the longest being 4 miles and the shortest 1¾ miles and as such they have been designed very much with families in mind.

The pubs from which each stroll commences have been selected with great care not only for their aesthetic appeal but because they provide excellent value for money. Times when food is available have been indicated in the individual pub descriptions as have general opening times where these are known. However, these are sometimes changed without notice. Therefore it is best to check beforehand by using the telephone number which is given at the end of each description. Also, where the menu is the subject of constant variation, only an outline of the type of food available is given. Again each pub can be contacted in order to obtain specific details.

Furthermore, it must be stressed that the pub car parks are only for patrons – and please check with the landlord that your car will not be in the way while you are your stroll. Alternative parking locatio when available, have been indicated in text.

A prime objective has been to prov direct, no-nonsense route descriptions each walk, coupled with a clear acco panying sketch map. For those requir more detail, the relevant OS Landran 1:50 000 map numbers are given.

Do not be afraid to venture out dur the winter months, for an excursion o cold, clear day when frost has hardened ground underfoot can be most rewardi especially when coupled with a warm drink and a hearty meal taken in pleas surroundings. However, if you wish enjoy the facilities of an inn following completion of a walk please remember leave muddy walking boots in your car. I also recommended that you carry a char of footwear if you are visiting a coun house or museum en route.

Finally, some words of thanks. As w previous surveys I have been accompan during the preparations for this book my mother – who has made a valu contribution to the finished work. K Mannion once again did an excellent job converting my handwriting into a typ manuscript. Thanks also go to all managers and landlords of the various p for taking time out to answer my ma questions.

James F. Edwa

Lymm
The Golden Fleece

MAP: OS LANDRANGER 109 (GR 683868)   **WALK 1**   **DISTANCE:** 3¼ MILES

DIRECTIONS TO START: LYMM IS MIDWAY BETWEEN WARRINGTON AND ALTRINCHAM WHICH ARE CONNECTED BY THE A56 ROAD. THE GOLDEN FLEECE IS SITUATED CLOSE TO THE VILLAGE CENTRE, NEAR THE CANAL. **PARKING:** IN THE PUB CAR PARK, WITH PERMISSION. ALTERNATIVELY, THERE IS A PUBLIC CAR PARK IN PEPPER STREET, WHICH IS ONLY A SHORT DISTANCE FROM THE INN.

Lymm is a mixture of appealing buildings, half-timbered houses and interesting shops. For such a small place there is also an abundance of eateries together with no less than five inns! The village has something to offer every age group. From the fascination of its buildings; the historical association with Britain's first canal; the delights of the flora and fauna to be seen at Lymm Dam; there are so many varied aspects crammed into a small geographical area. The walk takes you through the centre of the village prior to circumnavigating the picturesque waters of Lymm Dam, then continues along field paths and lanes to reach the towpath of the Bridgewater Canal for the stroll back to the village.

The Golden Fleece

This attractive inn is built on three levels where low ceilings and old brassware create an intimate atmosphere. A range of Greenalls beer and cask ales is on offer together with draught Strongbow cider. Food is served every lunchtime and evening as well as roast joints every Sunday lunchtime. There are varied starters and the main courses include steaks, chicken, mixed grills, chicken tikka masala and various seafood dishes. Vegetarian dishes are also available. The inn boasts a splendid canalside beer garden with a separate play area for children. Telephone: 01925 755538.

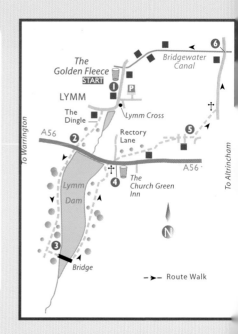

The Walk

① On leaving the inn turn right and follow the road away from the canal bridge and into the village centre with its mixture of interesting buildings. On the left, close to the head of Pepper Street, is Lymm Cross, an old sandstone monument which has been restored during recent years. The road turns sharply to the right where there is a small lake and a weir on the left. Turn left now, to enter the Dingle, and pass cottages, one of which is called Rock Cottage. Follow a macadam path through trees, which keeps parallel with a stream on the left and after 250 yards climb up a flight of steps to arrive at a crossing road.

② Walk straight across the road, taking care, to follow a well-trodden path which follows the edge of Lymm Dam. Over to the left, across the water, can be seen the square stone tower of St Mary's church. Keep along a well-defined path which stays close by the water. Further on, stay forward on the main path which takes you away from th[e] waterside. At the next junction of paths kee[p] forward again, in the same direction a[s] before. Arrive at a large, balustraded, ston[e] bridge which is on the left.

③ Cross the bridge, which seems far to[o] large just for pedestrian traffic, and then tu[rn] left to descend steps. Follow a well-define[d] footpath through trees, which is never to[o] far away from the water on the left. Emerg[e] from the trees and remain on the high[er] ground to fork left and then, bearing righ[t] descend through outcrops of sandstone. Pa[ss] in front of the churchyard and then be[ar] right to emerge onto a roadside paveme[nt] close by the church. Turn right and arri[ve] close by the Church Green Inn.

④ From the Church Green Inn cross t[he] road, taking care, and enter a fenced-in pa[th] which begins between cottages overlooki[ng] a small green close to the head of Rect[ory]

mm Cross

ne. This path begins at the side of mber 35. The path takes you to a facing ıd. Keep forward along the pavement and passing the entrance to a large house on e left called The Hatchings enter a crow path which leads past the back of uses and along the edge of a large field. here a path goes off to the left keep ward, in the same direction as before, and en pass the head of Orchard Avenue – ıich goes off to the left. Pass a wooden :e and go over a road constructed from lividual bricks. Pass another wooden gate l, again, go over a road which is built m individual bricks. On passing a further oden gate continue to where, just before end in a facing lane is arrived at, you turn t to enter a footpath.

The footpath runs between fences and :es you across fields in the direction of a ırch. Emerge onto a lane by the church l turn left to descend along the laneside pavement. Arrive at a bridge which carries the lane over a canal. Cross the bridge and then leave the lane to the left to arrive on the towpath of the canal.

⑥ Turn right along the towpath to stroll away from the bridge you have just walked over. Keep on, along the towpath, and shortly after passing Lymm Cruising Club, leave the canal to the right, just before a bridge is reached. Cross the bridge to arrive back in the village of Lymm.

PLACES OF INTEREST NEARBY

About 5 miles to the east of Lymm, and accessible via the A56, is the lovely estate of **Dunham Massey** with its magnificent hall and herds of fallow deer. Dunham Hall and Gardens are open every day of the week (except Thursdays and Fridays) 12 noon to 5 pm from April to October inclusive. The Deer Park is open all year. Telephone: 0161 9411025.

Sworton Heath
The Bears Paw

DIRECTIONS TO START: THE HAMLET OF SWORTON HEATH IS MIDWAY BETWEEN KNUTSFORD AND WARRINGTON – WHICH ARE CONNECTED BY THE A50 ROAD. THE BEARS PAW FRONTS ONTO THIS ROAD. **PARKING:** IN THE PUB CAR PARK, WITH PERMISSION. ALTERNATIVELY, DRIVE ALONG THE A50 IN THE DIRECTION OF WARRINGTON AND TURN LEFT INTO SWINEYARD LANE. AFTER ¾ MILE TURN LEFT INTO MOSS BROW LANE AND THEN LEFT AGAIN INTO MOSS LANE, WHERE, AFTER ABOUT 200 YARDS, THERE IS A PARKING VERGE ON THE LEFT (START WALK AT POINT 7).

Between High Legh and Arley there is an expanse of very attractive countryside where farms and cottages are to be found in abundance. These dwellings are linked by numerous, virtually traffic-free, lanes which provide the visitor on foot with a means of exploring the area at first hand. On leaving the Bears Paw, the initial section of the walk involves about a mile of cross-country tracks and paths, after which a series of lanes take you past some very attractive, if rather isolated, dwellings many of which have a history going back hundreds of years. The return leg of the walk involves a mixture of field paths and lanes which lead to a final cross-country path – after which a winding country lane takes you back to the Bears Paw.

The Bears Paw

A former coaching house which dates back to the 17th century, the inn has a pleasing ambience and offers a warm welcome to visitors. The enthusiastic owners are keen to develop the business and a larger restaurant is planned. Currently, the inn has a couple of cosy lounges – one of which is non-smoking – where Greenalls and Boddingtons cask ales and home-cooked food can be enjoyed. Locally grown produce is used to create many tempting dishes and the menu is varied and constantly changing. A wide selection of beers, ciders and soft drinks can be purchased. Open every day between 12 noon and 11 pm, meals are served from 12 noon to 3 pm and 6 pm to 9 pm Monday to Friday, and from 12 noon to 9 pm on Saturday and Sunday. There is an attractive beer garden and a children's play area as well as a purpose-built outside barbecue – which comes into its own during the summer months. Telephone: 01925 752573.

The Walk

) From the Bears Paw car park cross the road, taking care, and enter a macadam driveway. Pass a delightful brick and timber cottage on the right called Coopers Square and then follow a track between hedgerows. The track takes you past a sport pavilion and tennis courts. Where the track finishes go over a stile to enter a large field. Walk forward, bearing slightly right, and then go over a stile on reaching the far corner of the field.

) Turn left now, and follow a gently winding field edge, keeping a hedgerow on

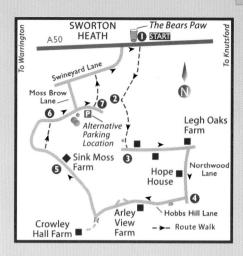

your immediate left. On reaching the field corner go over a stile at the side of a gate and then continue along a grassy track where there is a hedgerow on the immediate right. Pass through a gateway and continue along the track – there is a pond on the right now. The track leads to a stile which gives access to a lane.

③ Turn left along the lane. Pass a farm on the left and dwelling on the right, then keep on past the attractive Brown Owl Cottage. Arrive at a junction of lanes close by Legh Oaks Farm. Turn right here, in the direction of Great Budworth and Pickmere, to enter Northwood Lane. Shortly after passing Hope House arrive at Hobbs Hill Lane, which goes off to the right.

④ Enter Hobbs Hill Lane. Pass Hobbs Hill Cottage and Hobbs Hill Farm – where an attractive laneside water feature has been developed during recent years. A little further on, the lane takes you past Arley View Farm. Where the lane forks bear left and then bear left again at the next fork. Straight ahead, the M6 motorway can be seen. Follow the lane as it turns to the right

Arley Hall

near the entrance drive of Crowley Hall Farm. The lane stays roughly parallel with the motorway and leads to Sink Moss Farm – which has been developed into a private dwelling.

⑤ Remain on the lane for the next 200 yards and then go over a stile on the right which gives access to a field. Keep forward now and follow a straight path across the field to where, after 250 yards, you rejoin the lane. (This footpath cuts out a loop in the lane, which can be seen over to the left. You may wish to remain on the lane instead.)

⑥ Turn right along the lane – which leads past a number of dwellings. Shortly, there is a wood on the right and then a junction of lanes where Moss Brow Lane goes off to the left. Keep forward here, along Moss Lane. The lane gently bears to the right (the alternative parking location is here). About 300 yards from the previous junction of lanes there is a small earth-topped bridge at ground level – which passes over a dyke on the left.

⑦ Leave the lane here and cross th bridge to enter a field. Walk straight up th edge of the field keeping a hedgerow o your immediate left. Go over a stile an footbridge at the field corner and follo the edge of the next field – this time keep ing a hedgerow on your immediate right. stile at the end of the field gives access Swineyard Lane, where the way is righ Arrive at a junction. Cross the road, takir care, and turn right to follow the roadsic pavement back to the Bears Paw.

PLACES OF INTEREST NEARBY

About 3 miles to the south of Sworton Heath, ar accessible via the A50 and an unclassified roa that commences by High Legh Garden Centre ar which runs towards Great Budworth, are **Arle Hall and Gardens**. The hall is a fine example early Victorian 'Jacobean' style and is surrounde by 12 acres of gardens. There is also a gift sho and restaurant. The gardens are normally op during the afternoon between April ar September (closed on Mondays) but the openi times for the hall vary. Telephone: 01565 77735

Rostherne
The Swan Inn

MAP: OS LANDRANGER 109 (GR 732832)　　**WALK 3**　　**DISTANCE:** 3 MILES

DIRECTIONS TO START: THE SWAN INN AT BUCKLOW HILL IS SITUATED AT THE JUNCTION BETWEEN THE A556 AND A5034 KNUTSFORD ROAD, MIDWAY BETWEEN THE M56 AND M6 MOTORWAYS. **PARKING:** IN THE PUB CAR PARK, WITH PERMISSION. ALTERNATIVELY, THERE IS A SMALL PARKING AREA CLOSE BY THE PUB AT THE HEAD OF CICELEY MILL LANE.

On the fringes of the conurbation of Greater Manchester, the village of Rostherne is sometimes overlooked by those eager to search for something more distant, little realising that on their own doorstep is the very seclusion which they seek.

From the inn the route follows a lane into the village before joining a cross-country path to the outskirts of the great estate of Tatton Park. The return journey is by way of field paths – past a delightful lakeside setting – after which a lane leads back to the inn.

The Swan Inn

During recent years the Swan has developed into a large establishment although its origins as a coaching inn, serving the busy route between Manchester and Chester, are still obvious. The main road, the A556, follows the route of the Roman Watling Street and what is thought to be a stone road marker post from those times is let into a recess at the front of the inn. A comprehensive range of food and drink is available from 12 noon to 2.30 pm and from 6 pm to 9.30 pm every day. This includes sandwiches, bar meals and restaurant meals with all the trimmings. During the summer months benches and tables are provided for outside use. Telephone: 01565 830295.

The Walk

① On leaving the inn, turn left and enter Ciceley Mill Lane. After ½ mile, arrive at a junction of lanes in the centre of the village of Rostherne.

The main body of the village, with its post office and attractive cottages is to the right, whilst to the left access can be gained to the church confines. The church has a sandstone tower (1742) which replaced an earlier steeple (1533) and contains the tombs of the Egerton family of Tatton Park. From the rear of the church there is a fine view to Rostherne Mere – which is over 100 feet deep and is kept as a nature reserve.

Having looked around the village and its church, leave by the lane along which you arrived and after 150 yards arrive at a stile which is set in a hedgerow on the left.

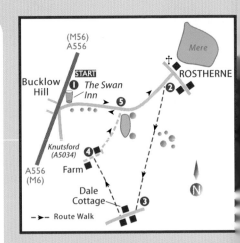

② Cross the stile and enter a large field. Bear right and walk to the far corner of the field. Go through a kissing gate and keep on, in the same direction as before, across the next field. Pass through another kissing gate to enter a very large field. Follow well-defined path in the direction of buildings which can be seen at the far side of the field. When you are halfway across the field Tatton Hall comes into view at the end of an avenue of trees. Emerge from the field and arrive at a crossing road.

③ Turn right and, after 150 yards, pass Dale Cottage. Leave the road to the right now, over a stile at the side of a field gate. The path hugs the garden hedge of Dale Cottage at first, and then a straight length of path leads to a stile in a crossing hedgerow. Go over the stile and cross the next field in the same direction as before. Pass close to a telephone pole and then go over a stile at the side of a field gate. Cross the next field and then go over a stile to arrive on a crossing drive, where there is a farm on the left and a dwelling on the right.

The attractive lake near Rostherne

) Turn right and follow the drive past the welling. Immediately on passing the welling turn left and descend to pass over stream. Go over a stile here and enter an undulating field. Bear right and climb up a ass bank and then cross level terrain to go er a stile in a crossing fence. Keep on, to here, after a few more yards, a splendid ene opens up ahead where there is a lake th a scenic backdrop of woods. The otpath descends over stiles and takes you ose to the water's edge. Pass over a stile at e side of a gate and emerge onto a lane.

⑤ You are now back on part of your initial route. Turn left and follow the lane back to the Swan Inn – which is ¼ mile away.

PLACES OF INTEREST NEARBY

Tatton Park Estate, which can be reached along the A5034 in the direction of Knutsford and then along a minor road (signposted), gives a glimpse of a way of life which is hundreds of years old. There is a mansion and hall, a working farm and delightful gardens. Telephone: 01565 750250.

Hatton
The Hatton Arms

MAP: OS LANDRANGER 108 (GR 599824)   **WALK 4**   **DISTANCE:** 3¼ MILES

DIRECTIONS TO START: HATTON LIES ON THE B5356 STRETTON TO DARESBURY ROAD, MIDWAY BETWEEN THE A49 AND A56, LESS THAN 5 MILES TO THE SOUTH OF WARRINGTON. **PARKING:** IN THE PUB CAR PARK, WITH PERMISSION.

The very first mention of Hatton was during the early years of the reign of King Henry III, when the township was given to William son of Hothy of Hatton. Over the ensuing years the village has not expanded very much and is largely a mixture of cottages spread out along the road to Warrington. Between the First and Second World Wars there are records relating to an annual influx of potato-picking gangs of Irishmen who worked with the villagers digging and bagging the local crop. feature of the village was that, up to t beginning of the 20th century, it had piped water supply and its community h to rely on wells which were scattered and around the village. The route of t walk takes you past a number of cottag before striking out across country follow a scenic field path over pasture la and through woods. The return leg along a road, a cross-country lane and track – on the way back to Hatton.

The Hatton Arms

Described on a map of 1873 as the Red Lion, this converted 17th century cottage presents an appealing aspect with its cobbled entrance and colourful window-boxes. Inside low beams and a cosy atmosphere create a pleasing ambience. Owned by Scottish and Newcastle Breweries, the range of beers on offer also includes products from Greenalls, Theakston and John Smith's – plus a variety of lagers and soft drinks. The inn offers light snacks and bar meals as well as a full restaurant service. The range and type of food on offer is substantial with two different bar and restaurant menus operating at any one time as well as a comprehensive specials board. The inn is open every day between 11.30 am and 11 pm (Sundays 12 noon to 11 pm) and food is served at lunchtimes between 12 noon and 2 pm and during the evenings between 6.30 pm and 9 pm. When the weather is fine benches are arranged on the cobbled area at the front of the inn and there is also a separate beer garden. Telephone: 01925 730314.

The Walk

On leaving the inn, turn right and follow the roadside pavement along Warrington Road. Pass various dwellings. Where the pavement finishes cross to the other side of the road and continue. Pass Hatton Hall Farm and a mixture of cottages. On passing the entrance to Bluecoat Farm the pavement finishes. Continue along the roadside for a further 200 yards or where, on the left, there is a kissing gate by a sign which says 'Moore 2 miles'.

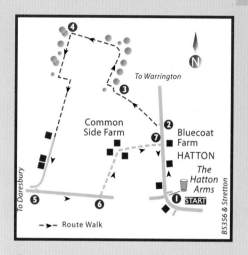

② Leave the roadside here, and pass through the kissing gate to enter a field. Walk forward for 40 yards, and then turn right to go through another gate. Gradually bear away from a hedge on the right hand side, which is interspersed with large trees, and after 200 yards pass through a kissing gate in a crossing hedgerow. Walk straight up the middle of a large field and on reaching the end of it arrive at a kissing gate which is set in a fence in front of a wood.

③ Go through the kissing gate and follow a well-defined footpath through the wood. Pass over a flat footbridge and wind and climb. Emerge from the trees through a kissing gate. Turn right and follow the edge of a large field, keeping a fence and the wood on your immediate right. Follow the fence when it turns to the left and gradually climb along the field edge. Immediately after the point where the trees finish go through a kissing gate and follow a field edge, in the same general direction as before. On reaching level terrain there are long views across to Warrington and beyond. Keep on, to arrive at trees – where there is a junction of paths.

One of Hatton's delightful cottages

④ Turn left here, to follow a field edge, keeping the trees on your immediate right. On reaching the end of the field, go through a kissing gate and turn left to walk up to the corner of the next field. Turn right now and keep along the field edge. Pass through a kissing gate at the side of a field gate and keep on along a hedged-in track. Shortly, you will pass a stable block, after which the track has become a lane. Pass dwellings, and where the lane bends to the right, keep forward along a short length of path to arrive at a crossing road.

⑤ Turn left and follow the roadside as it descends, and then climbs, for ½ mile, to arrive at the entrance drive of Common Side Farm, which is on the left.

⑥ Enter the macadam drive, which is slightly raised above the field on the left. Arrive at the farm, pass through the farm-

yard, turning right, and then pass throug[h] small gate at the side of a field gate. Foll[ow] a track away from the farm. The track le[ads] to a kissing gate which gives access t[o] crossing road opposite Bluecoat Farm.

⑦ Turn right and follow the roads[ide] pavement. You are now back on part [of] your original route. Keep on, to arrive b[ack] at the Hatton Arms.

PLACES OF INTEREST NEARBY

A little over 1 mile along the road wh[ich] commences directly opposite the entrance to [the] Hatton Arms is the interesting village [of] **Daresbury** and people come from distant pla[ces] to visit it. The reason for their pilgrimage is t[hat] Lewis Carroll, the author of *Alice's Adventu[res] in Wonderland*, was born here, and all over [the] village there are reminders of the colou[rful] characters depicted in his stories. There is als[o a] Lewis Carroll Centre.

Morley Green
The Range

| MAP: OS LANDRANGER 109 (GR 833814) | WALK 5 | DISTANCE: 2½ MILES |

DIRECTIONS TO START: THE BODDINGTON ARMS IS JUST UNDER ONE MILE ALONG THE A538 FROM THE CENTRE OF WILMSLOW, IN THE DIRECTION OF ALTRINCHAM. **PARKING:** IN THE PUB CAR PARK, WITH PERMISSION. ALTERNATIVELY, THERE IS A PUBLIC CAR PARK OPPOSITE THE PUB ENTRANCE ON RACECOURSE ROAD.

The outward leg of today's walk starts from the Range, a pub known until recently as the Boddington Arms. The cuit takes in a section of the Bollin Valley 'ay prior to reaching the tiny hamlet of orley Green – which lives up to its name with its attractive village green. The route then follows a path across Lindow Moss where, in 1984, the well-preserved body of a Celtic Iron Age man who came to be known as 'Lindow Pete' was discovered. The final section of the walk is along well-defined paths and tracks.

The Range

The pub is a large establishment with a bright interior where a wide choice of food and drink can be consumed in comfort. Boddingtons and Higsons supply the beer whilst there is also a superb selection of spirits and liqueurs, together with a comprehensive range of wines. The menu is extensive – running to nine pages of delicious offerings. There are assorted starters, steaks and grills, salad platters, chicken and fish together with a 'Specials Table'. Puddings, desserts and ice cream sundaes are also available. The inn welcomes families and children are well catered for with their own menu. Food is served from 12 noon to 2.30 pm and from 5.30 pm to 10.30 pm Monday to Friday. On Saturday and Sunday food is available between 12 noon and 10 pm. During the summer months benches and tables are made available for use in front of the pub. Telephone: 01625 525849.

The Walk

① On leaving the pub, cross the facing car park and turn left to follow a roadside pavement. Keep on, past Kings Road and Greaves Road, and shortly after passing a garage turn left to enter Mobberley Road. After 120 yards, arrive at a bungalow on the left called Sandiway.

② Leave the lane to the right here, where a footpath sign points towards Morley Green. You have now joined a section of the Bollin Valley Way. Follow a well-defined path along a field edge, keeping a hedgerow on the immediate right, and then pass through a gate. The path runs between hedgerows now. Keep forward over a cross ing track and follow the path to emerg onto a lane.

③ Walk straight across the lane and over a facing stile to enter a field. Wa straight up the centre of the field and th pass over a narrow grassy area to emer into a large, undulating field. Keep alo the right hand edge of the field, keeping fence and hedgerow interspersed with tre on the immediate right. Pass through a g in a crossing hedge and then go over a st near dwellings. Follow a narrow hedged path which leads to a crossing road.

④ Turn left and follow the roadside pa ment to where, after ¼ mile, you arrive the green in the hamlet of Morley Gree

⑤ Enter a track which commences dire ly opposite Morley Green Road (the r you have just walked along) at the side bungalow called Fourways. After 150 ya there is a junction of ways. Keep forw here to pass to the right of a dwelling ca Sunnyside. Pass through a facing gate follow a path through trees.

uarry Bank Mill

) Emerge from the trees to follow a well-
efined path which gradually climbs up a
llside over open scrubland. Reach the
est of the hill and keep forward, ignoring
path which goes off to the left. Gradually
escend and arrive at a junction of paths
st before facing trees are reached.

) Turn left to follow a well-defined path
d after 200 yards walk across a broad
assy path to descend onto a track which
kes you past well-tended allotments. Pass
netal gate at the side of a dwelling called
wers Folly and follow a facing macadam
ive which turns to the left and becomes a

gravel track. Keep forward where a track
goes off to the left and arrive at a crossing
road. Turn right here to follow the roadside
pavement back to the Range pub which is
200 yards away.

PLACES OF INTEREST NEARBY

About 3 miles from the Boddington Arms, and
accessible via the A538 to Wilmslow and then A34
and B5166 to Styal, is the award winning
museum at **Quarry Bank Mill**, where a 200 year
old working environment has been recreated.
Telephone: 01625 527468.

Great Warford
The Frozen Mop

DIRECTIONS TO START: KNUTSFORD AND ALDERLEY EDGE ARE CONNECTED BY THE B5085 ROAD. MIDWAY BETWEEN THESE TWO PLACES IS THE HAMLET OF KNOLLS GREEN WHERE THERE IS AN INN CALLED THE BIRD IN HAND. ABOUT 250 YARDS FROM THIS INN IN THE DIRECTION OF KNUTSFORD IS FAULKNERS LANE, WHERE A SIGN POINTS TOWARDS THE METHODIST CHURCH. DRIVE ALONG FAULKNERS LANE, AND IN LESS THAN ½ MILE ARRIVE AT THE FROZEN MOP. **PARKING:** IN THE PUB CAR PARK, WITH PERMISSION.

This delightful stroll crosses lush green meadows and follows quiet country lanes where the route is never too far away from the burbling waters of Mobberley Brook. From the pub a cross-country path links up with Paddock Hill Lane which in turn lea past some attractive country dwelling Another series of cross-country paths and lan are then followed for the return leg of t journey back to Great Warford.

The Frozen Mop

The pub takes its unusual name from an incident when a former landlady discovered that the mop and bucket of water which she kept at the front of the building had frozen solid one cold winter's morning. Extended during recent years, the pub has an attractive interior where Whitbread ales are available. The variety of food on offer is amazing; apart from traditional English fare there is a range of Italian and Indian dishes. Food is served every day between 11.30 am and 10 pm and can be eaten in the restaurant or taken as bar meals. There is an indoor and outdoor play area for children and a large beer garden. Telephone: 01565 873234.

The Walk

① On leaving the pub turn right along Faulkners Lane and after 250 yards go over a stile on the left which is opposite a dwelling called The Headmasters House. Follow the edge of a large field, keeping a hedgerow on your immediate left. Pass over a sturdy wooden footbridge, which takes you over Mobberley Brook, and turn right to follow a well-defined path where there is a fence on the immediate left. Pass over a couple of stiles. The path leads to a crossing road through an outbuilding.

② Cross the road, taking care, and go over a stile to enter a field. Follow the field edge, keeping a hedgerow on your immediate right, and after 150 yards go over a stile. Bear left now, keeping a fence and trees on your immediate left. Pass over a stile in a crossing fence and keep on to arrive at the end of the field. Go over two stiles in quick succession and arrive onto a crossing lane.

③ Turn right along the lane. Keep on, past dwellings, and on passing a large bungalow called Annapurna keep right along Paddock Hill Lane. Shortly after passing the attractive Damson Tree Cottage there is a junction of lanes near a telephone box. Keep right here, and then right again, to continue along Paddock Hill Lane.

④ About 50 yards after passing the imposing entrance gate of Rosemary Cottage leave the lane to the right, opposite Maple Farm, to go over a stile. Follow a grassy track along the edge of a field, keeping a ditch and hedgerow on your immediate right. Pass over a stile at the side of a gate and immediately pass over another stile, to walk in the direction of a farm which can be seen straight ahead. After 80 yards go over a stile and walk towards the farm, keeping a fence on your immediate right. A stile at the end of a building gives access to a paved area where there is a wall on the left. There is a dwelling on the right here but keep forward and bear left to join

On the route

a macadam drive. Follow the drive to arrive at a crossing road.

⑤ Cross the road, taking care, and go over a stile to enter a large, undulating field. Bear left and after 150 yards descend into a hollow. Bear right. There is a winding brook on the left here. Gradually converge with a hedgerow on the right and then go over a stile which is in a crossing hedgerow. Bear left now and descend, then pass over a stream via a plank-bridge and stiles. Climb forward into the next field and walk towards a dwelling which can be seen straight ahead. Go over a stile which gives access to a crossing lane.

⑥ Turn right and follow the lane over Mobberley Brook. After about ½ mile, th lane passes between farm buildings to junction. Turn right here, and the immediately right again, to enter Faulkne Lane. Follow the lane back to the Froze Mop, which is a little over ¼ mile away.

PLACES OF INTEREST NEARBY

About 3 miles from the Frozen Mop, an accessible via the B5085, is the town of Alderle Edge. To its eastern side, and reached by drivin through the town along the A34 in the directic of Congleton and then turning left to climb for mile along the B5087 in the direction Macclesfield, is the elevated viewpoint known **'The Edge'**. Here there are tree-lined walks ar long views across the Cheshire plain.

Willaston-in-Wirral
The Pollard Inn

MAP: OS LANDRANGER 117 (GR 329777) | **WALK 7** | **DISTANCE:** 3½ MILES

DIRECTIONS TO START: WILLASTON IS ON THE B5133, 8 MILES TO THE NORTH-WEST OF CHESTER AND 1 MILE TO THE EAST OF THE A540 CHESTER TO HOYLAKE ROAD. THE POLLARD INN IS CLOSE TO THE CENTRE OF THE VILLAGE, OFF HADLOW ROAD. **PARKING:** THERE IS A LARGE PUBLIC CAR PARK CLOSE BY THE INN.

One of the oldest villages on the Wirral Peninsula, Willaston is a mix of the old and the new. At its heart is the village green, close to which is the imposing Willaston Old Hall constructed during the 17th century and whose beautiful gardens are occasionally opened to the public during summertime. The village also possesses a windmill, the tallest in Wirral, which was built in 1800 and once provided employment for 40 people, but has not been operational since 1930. During 1866 a railway track which ran between Hooton and West Kirby was completed and this ran to the west of the village. The railway closed in 1956 and its route has been turned into a linear footpath known as the Wirral Way. The walk utilises part of the Wirral Way before joining an attractive lane which in turn leads to a wooded track. Field paths are then crossed to the windmill, after which a further cross-country path takes you back to Willaston.

The Pollard Inn

Known as the Hidden Inn on the Wirral, The Pollard Inn is a picture-postcard hostelry which was formerly a farmhouse dating back to the 14th century. During the Civil War (1642–49) a cannonball was fired which, during recent years, was removed from one of the walls. The inn is a Greenalls house and serves Original cask conditioned bitter brewed in the tradition of the first 27 barrels of ale produced at Wilderspool Brewery on 10th January 1787. Bar snacks are available Monday to Saturday from 12 noon to 2.30 pm and 5 pm to 7 pm; Sundays from 12 noon through to 7 pm. Full restaurant meals – where the choices are really comprehensive – are available from 12 noon to 2.30 pm and from 7 pm onwards every day. The inn has a cocktail bar and an attractive conservatory. Outside, there is a patio area, a beer garden and a children's play area. Accommodation is available if required. Telephone: 0151 3274615.

The Walk

① On leaving the inn, walk back to Hadlow Road and cross it to enter the facing Smithy Lane. Turn immediately right here, at the side of a house called Westbourne, to follow a rough lane. The lane takes you past various dwellings. At a junction keep forward and pass Home-leigh. The lane becomes a gravel track between hedges. Keep on past a path which goes to Adfalent Lane, and then keep to the left of a dwelling to follow a narrow hedged-in path. The path leads to the Wirral Way.

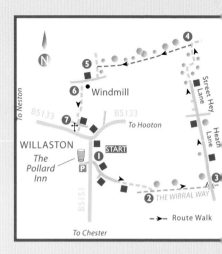

② Turn left now to walk along the rou[te] of the former railway line which used [to] connect Hooton with West Kirby. Af[ter] almost ½ mile, arrive at a bridge. Do n[ot] pass under this bridge, but turn left [to] follow a gravel track which joins Hea[th] Lane.

③ Turn left along the lane, which tak[es] you past very attractive dwellings. Keep o[n] past Barford Grange and arrive at [a] crossing road. Walk straight across t[he] road, taking care, and enter the faci[ng] Street Hey Lane. Keep on past Beech H[ey] and Field Hey Lanes. The lane narro[ws] and is skirted by large trees. On passing [a] dwelling called Woodhome the la[ne] becomes a track which goes through tre[es.] Follow the track as it turns to the right. [A] little further on, the track turns to the le[ft.] There are a couple of ponds on the l[eft] now. The track has become a path throu[gh] trees.

④ Do not follow the path as it turns [to] the right, but leave it to the left, to go ov[er] a plank-bridge and stile which give acce[ss] to a field. Follow the field edge, keepi[ng]

The windmill at Willaston

ees on your immediate right, and then go ver a plank-bridge and stile at the field rner. The path is now fenced. Emerge from the fenced-in path at a plank-bridge and stile and follow a well-defined path along the edge ~a large field, with a hedge and trees on your immediate right. On reaching the end of the field go over a stile and descend three stone steps to arrive onto a track.

) Turn left and follow the track through es. Arrive at a crossing lane opposite a row cottages. Turn right here. On the immediate left now, is Willaston Windmill which has, during recent years, been converted to a private dwelling. About 150 yards after ssing the windmill, arrive at a stile on the t where an old fashioned footpath sign says ublic Footpath to Willaston'.

Leave the lane and go over the stile. he path follows a field edge where there is ence on the left. After 200 yards, go over

a stile and follow a narrow fenced-in path. Shortly, a kissing gate gives access to a sports field. Follow the left hand edge of the sports field and then turn left to follow a gravel path past Jackson Pond. The path takes you between dwellings and leads to a lane opposite church confines.

⑦ Turn left, and then right, to follow a path which runs alongside the church confines. The path leads to a crossing road. Cross the road, taking care, and turn left, to follow the roadside pavement. You are now back in the village of Willaston. Turn next right to enter Hadlow Road. A few more strides take you back to the inn.

PLACES OF INTEREST NEARBY
Just over 2½ miles to the south-west of Willaston are the extensive 62 acre **Ness Gardens** – which are a delight throughout all the seasons of the year. Telephone: 0151 3530123.

Ollerton
The Dun Cow

MAP: OS LANDRANGER 118 (GR 775769)   **WALK 8**   **DISTANCE:** 3½ MILES

DIRECTIONS TO START: OLLERTON STRADDLES THE A537 KNUTSFORD TO CHELFORD ROAD 2 MILES FROM THE CENTRE OF KNUTSFORD. THE DUN COW FRONTS ONTO THIS ROAD. **PARKING:** IN THE PUB CAR PARK, WITH PERMISSION.

The area to the south-east of Knutsford is dairy farming country. Apart from lush green pastures which support this traditional way of life, there is also a mixture of woodland glades and streams which are a haven for wildlife. The outward loop of the walk heads north towards Mobberley before swinging south to cross the Knutsford t Chelford road near Ollerton Hall. This sectio includes tracks, field paths and bridleways. Th return leg follows field paths across ric agricultural land where there are numero stiles to negotiate.

The Dun Cow

Situated close to where a turnpike gate once stood, the Dun Cow used to cater for travellers on horseback and the inn which we see today still retains many features from those far-off times – including exposed beams both in the lounge and restaurant. Scottish and Newcastle beers are served and there is also an extensive wine list. Apart from the restaurant, delicious bar meals can be consumed in the lounge area. There is a set menu together with specials and vegetarian meals which are served every day. Food is available from 12 noon to 2 pm and 6 pm to 9 pm Monday to Friday, and from 12 noon to 9 pm at weekends. Telephone: 01565 633093.

he Walk

) Enter a track on the opposite side of ₁e pub to the car park entrance and pass ₁rough a gate. On passing to the right of ₁other gate turn left and right between ₁ildings. A straight length of grassy track ₁ads to a facing gate. Go over a stile at the ₁de of this gate and continue along the ₁ack. There are ponds on both sides of the ₁ack. Where the track turns to the right to ₁field gate, go over a facing stile.

) Follow a field edge, keeping a ditch and ₁hedgerow on your immediate right. Pass ₁rough a gap at the next field corner and ₁ep on along the edge of the next field. A ₁ank-bridge and stile at the field corner ₁ve access to a wooded area. The path runs ₁ong the left hand side of a wide grassy ₁₁a which cuts through the trees where ₁ere is a meandering brook over to the ₁ht. Cross a sturdy footbridge and follow

a facing path through trees to emerge into a large field over a stile.

③ With the stile at your back, walk straight across the facing field to where, after about 250 yards, you arrive at a crossing hedge and fence. Turn right and after a few strides go over a stile which is to the left of a field gate. Walk straight across the next field, keeping a hedgerow on your left about 100 yards away. A stile in a crossing hedge gives access to the next field.

④ Bear slightly right now, gradually moving away from a hedgerow on the left, and cross the field, passing to the left of a clump of trees. Keep on, in the same direction, aiming about 60 yards to the right of a gate which can be seen in a crossing hedgerow. Go over a stile at the end of the field to arrive on a lane.

⑤ Turn right, cross a bridge, and then go over a stile on the left to enter a large, undulating field. The path bears slightly right and is never too far away from a brook on the left. About 50 yards after passing an earth-topped low level bridge, go over a pair of footbridges and adjacent stiles. Turn right now and after 120 yards go over a footbridge and stiles to enter the next field. Keep to the right of a sunken tree-lined hollow and then pass over another stile. Keep on, in the same direction as before, aiming just to the right of a dwelling which can be seen about ¼ mile away straight ahead. A stile in a crossing hedgerow gives access to the Knutsford to Chelford road.

⑥ Turn left and then almost immediately cross the road, taking care, to go over a stile in the opposite hedgerow. Walk straight across the facing field and pass over a stile in front of a dwelling. Turn right along a lane and after only 50 yards arrive at a junction.

⑦ Go through a facing field gate to follow a path which hugs a hedgerow and fence on the right. Cross a stream via a pair of stiles and keep on, to then pass over a footbridge and stiles which are set close to trees. Follow the edge of the next field to where, after 80 yards, there is a stile at the field corner. Turn right on crossing this stile and follow a field edge, keeping a fence on your immediate right. Turn left at the field corner and keep on, now with a hedgerow on your right. On reaching the field corner go over a stile. There is a plank-bridge here.

⑧ Do not cross the plank-bridge but go over an adjacent stile on the immediate right. Turn left now to follow the field edge and after only 60 yards go over a plank bridge and stile. Cut across the corner of the next field to where, after only 40 yards there is another stile to negotiate. Turn left to follow a winding field edge and after about 90 yards go over a stile. Turn right along a grassy track where there is hedgerow on the immediate right. After 100 yards pass over a stile at the side of gate. The track bears to the left and then after a further 30 yards, turns to the right

⑨ Do not follow the track as it turns to the right but go through a facing gate. Keep along the field edge for 70 yards and then turn right to gradually climb for 120 yards to pass over a stile. Converge with fence and trees on the left. The path leads to a gate which gives access to a road. Cross the road, taking care, and turn left to follow the roadside pavement. Pass Woods Close and Marthall Lane, at which point the Dun Cow can be seen straight ahead. A few more strides take you back to the car park.

Plumley
The Golden Pheasant

DIRECTIONS TO START: PLUMLEY IS 3 MILES TO THE SOUTH-WEST OF KNUTSFORD. FROM THE A556, A 1 MILE DRIVE ALONG A ROAD WHICH COMMENCES AT THE SIDE OF THE SMOKER INN LEADS TO THE GOLDEN PHEASANT. **PARKING:** IN THE PUB CAR PARK, WITH PERMISSION.

Situated in the midst of an active farming community, Plumley maintains a rural atmosphere. Over the years there has been some confusion relating to various ways of spelling its name. During the 18th century it was called Plumbley, the 'b' being dropped in the 19th century, but reappearing again until finally being banned in 1944. The area is traversed by a meandering stream called the Peover Eye – which is stocked with trout, whilst its banks are home to many different species of wildlife. During today's walk you will cross this stream a couple of times on a jaunt which is a delightful mixture of field paths, tracks and lanes, to gain an insight into the country life of an interesting corner of the county.

The Golden Pheasant

The inn is set in 6 acres of grounds and there is an outside bar beside an adjacent bowling green. A large establishment, food and drink is provided to suit every taste and food times are 12 noon to 2.30 pm and 5.30 pm to 9.30 pm every day. The beer is provided by J.W. Lees of Middleton, which is complemented by a comprehensive range of ciders and soft drinks. The inn has a separate restaurant offering a variety of starters and an extremely wide choice of main meals, including lamb rump, chicken, rump steak, fillets of lamb and beef and a choice of fish dishes. There is a selection of side orders and a range of tempting puddings. A traditional lunch is always served on Sunday and there is a special meal for Senior Citizens. The inn can provide en-suite accommodation if required. Telephone: 01565 722261.

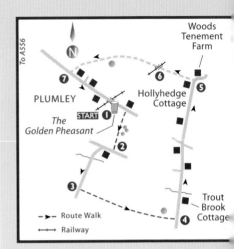

The Walk

① On leaving the inn, turn right and follow the roadside. After 200 yards, and opposite the entrance to a farm, go over a stile on the right. The path runs between a fence and a row of conifer trees. After 100 yards, go over a stile at the side of a gate and continue along a field edge, keeping a hedgerow on your immediate left. Go over a stile and plank-bridge at the field corner. There is a pond on the left here. The path runs across the next field and stays parallel with a hedge on the left. Go over a stile which is at the side of a gate and arrive on a crossing lane.

② Turn right, and pass Trout Hall Farm, to arrive at a junction. Turn left here, in the direction of Lach Dennis. The lane take you over the Peover Eye. About 220 yard further on, arrive at a stile on the left whic is at the side of a field gate.

③ Go over the stile and follow the edge a field, where there is a hawthorn hedge the immediate right. Pass over a footbridg on reaching the end of the field. Wa forward and then pass to the end of hedgerow which goes off to the right. Ke on to cross a large field, aiming about yards to the right of a thatched cotta which can be seen about 300 yards aw On nearing the end of the field, pass clo to an isolated tree and then go over a st at the side of a gate, to enter a lane.

④ Turn left along the lane and pass Tro Brook Cottage. Cross the Peover Eye on again and keep on past a lane which g off to the left. Arrive at a crossing roa Keep straight on here, taking care, to en the facing Pinfold Lane. Follow this la for almost ½ mile, to arrive at a track wh goes off to the left immediately on pass Hollyhedge Cottage, and in front Woods Tenement Farm.

ollyhedge Cottage

) Leave the lane to the left here and ter the track. A gravel track becomes a assy track between hedges and leads to a ing gate. Go over a stile on the left here, enter a large field. Turn right and follow field edge. Arrive at a stile which leads to the railway.

Extreme caution is required now. ease follow the advice given on the rning sign and stop, look and listen for sign of a train before crossing to the er side of the lines – where a stile gives ess to a field. Follow the field edge and, er 60 yards, go over a stile at the side of ate to enter the adjacent field. Turn right walk to a stile which can be seen about) yards away at the junction of two lges. On crossing this stile bear slightly to the next stile which can be seen ut 200 yards away in a crossing hedge rees. Go over the stile and follow a path

along the edge of the next two fields and cross a further stile. As you reach the end of the next field a stile at its corner gives access to a narrow path which runs along the end of gardens close to property on the left. Emerge from the path and arrive at a crossing road.

⑦ Turn left and follow the roadside pavement past Plumley Village Hall. Keep on past Malt Kiln Road. Pass over the railway lines, via the roadbridge, and arrive back at the Golden Pheasant.

PLACES OF INTEREST NEARBY
About 3 miles from the Golden Pheasant, and reached via the A556 and A5033 towards Knutsford, is the splendid mansion of **Tabley House**. Built in 1769, the mansion's state rooms house a famous collection of early 19th century paintings. Telephone: 01565 750151 for opening times.

Crowton
The Hare and Hounds

DIRECTIONS TO START: CROWTON IS MIDWAY BETWEEN WEAVERHAM AND KINGSLEY WHICH ARE CONNECTED BY THE B5153 ROAD. THE HARE AND HOUNDS FRONTS ONTO THIS ROAD IN THE CENTRE OF THE VILLAGE. **PARKING:** IN THE PUB CAR PARK, WITH PERMISSION. ALTERNATIVELY, DRIVE ALONG THE B5153 IN THE DIRECTION OF KINGSLEY AND TURN NEXT RIGHT INTO A LANE CALLED CREEWOOD COMMON. AFTER ½ MILE ARRIVE AT AINSWORTH LANE, WHICH GOES OFF TO THE RIGHT. LEAVE THE CAR ON THE LEFT HERE, WHERE THERE IS A WIDE GRASS VERGE (START WALK AT POINT 6).

Crowton is an ancient place. Up to the middle of the 13th century it was close by the meeting place of the Hundred of Roelau – one of the eight Anglo-Saxon administrative areas of the county. During the 16th and 17th centuries crowds gathered in the fields near the village for the playing of a boisterous game known as 'Prisoners' Bars'. There are many old stone houses in the village and there has been a working mill since the Middle Ages. The walk takes you away fro the village through rolling farmland wh there are long views across the Weaver val and towards the hills near Frodsham. Initia the route is along field paths and tracks to outskirts of Acton Bridge, prior to a gen descent into the Weaver valley along a seclu lane. The return leg of the walk is along qu country lanes which lead back to Crowton.

The Hare and Hounds

In the style of a house, this attractive inn can trace a history going back over 300 years and this is reflected in the interior where there is a wealth of low beams and old fashioned inglenooks and fittings. A variety of wines and spirits, beers and lagers are on offer together with a multitude of soft drinks. There is a very attractive restaurant and meals are usually provided on Wednesday to Monday, lunchtime and evening although, due to the inn's popularity, it is advisable to check availability in advance. Outside you will find an appealing beer garden and two pet goats! Telephone: 01928 788851.

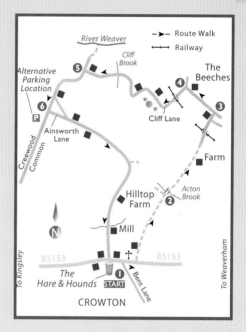

The Walk

1 On leaving the inn turn right, pass Bent Lane and follow the roadside pavement along Station Road. Across the road, on the left, is the tiny building of Christ Church. Where the pavement terminates turn left and cross the road, taking care, to enter Church Walk. After 50 yards of macadam keep forward through a facing gate to enter a field. Follow a track, keeping a hedgerow on your immediate left. Pass through a gate in the field corner and gradually descend along the edge of the next field, again keeping a hedgerow on your immediate left. On reaching the bottom of the gradual descent there is a junction of paths.

Keep forward now, to cross Acton Brook, and follow a well-defined path which climbs between hedgerows. The path levels out and becomes a track. Pass close to a farm and keep on along a facing lane which shortly crosses railway lines via a bridge. Pass Rookery Cottages, and keep on past Orchard Avenue, to arrive at a junction of lanes close by Acton Bridge Methodist church.

3 Turn left and follow the laneside pavement. Keep on past Pear Tree Lane and Cliff Cottage. On passing a house on the right called The Beeches there is a junction of lanes.

4 Turn left here, to follow Cliff Lane. This lane, which gradually descends, is a fine platform for long views ahead to the rolling hills behind Frodsham. Pass under the railway and follow the lane as it turns to the right. The lane takes you past semi-detached dwellings and then turns sharply to the right between Field House and Acton Cliff Farm. Over to the right, shortly, can be seen the impressive Dutton Viaduct which carries the railway across the river Weaver. This structure is 1,400 feet in

The river Weaver

length and was opened on 4 July 1837. Records tell us that it was built 'without loss to life or limb'. Pass a pumping station and follow the lane over Cliff Brook. The lane takes you past a couple of dwellings and leads to a junction of lanes. (The way is to the left but you may wish to turn right to have a look at the river Weaver before continuing your stroll. The water's edge is only 150 yards away and is reached by following the lane past ·a row of attractive cottages and then turning right to cross a footbridge which gives access to a riverside path.)

⑤ Turn left at the junction and follow a lane as it winds and climbs. On reaching level terrain there is a fork. Keep right here and after 250 yards arrive at Ainsworth Lane which goes off to the left (this is the alternative parking location).

⑥ Enter Ainsworth Lane and keep forward where there is a joining lane on t left. The lane takes you through t scattered hamlet of Ainsworth, which is pleasing mixture of cottages and farms. (leaving the dwellings behind, the lane tu to the right. Follow it past Hilltop Fa and then descend to the industrial buildi of Crowton Mill. There has been a mill this site for centuries. Follow a rai laneside pavement now, which takes y back to the centre of the village of Crow opposite the Hare and Hounds.

PLACES OF INTEREST NEARBY

About 5 miles to the east of Crowton, a accessible via the B5153 is the town of Northw – where Britain's only **Salt Museum** relates fascinating story of Cheshire's oldest industry. route is signposted on approaching the town. museum is open every day except Mono Tuesday to Friday 10 am to 5 pm and at weeke 2 pm to 5 pm. Telephone: 01606 41331.

Alvanley
The White Lion

MAP: OS LANDRANGER 117 (GR 497740) | **WALK 11** | **DISTANCE:** 3 MILES

DIRECTIONS TO START: THE B5393 RUNS GENERALLY NORTH TO SOUTH AND CONNECTS THE A56 AT FRODSHAM WITH THE A54 TO THE SOUTH OF ASHTON. THE B5393 CUTS THROUGH ALVANLEY 3 MILES FROM FRODSHAM, AND THE WHITE LION IS CLOSE TO THE CENTRE OF THE VILLAGE OPPOSITE ST JOHN'S CHURCH. **PARKING:** IN THE PUB CAR PARK, WITH PERMISSION.

Rising to the south of Frodsham and Helsby are the Overton Hills – where there are long panoramic views over the ersey Estuary. These hills, which were rmed over a million years ago, consist of red, llow and brown sandstone and rise to a ight approaching 400 feet. On the fringes of ese hills is the compact village of Alvanley – hich is at the heart of an attractive area of fields, woods and rolling countryside. The walk initially follows a road out of the village after which tracks and field paths are utilised for a gradual cross-country descent before turning along a grassy track which in turn leads to a quiet country lane. A gentle climb along the lane takes you back to the outskirts of Alvanley for the final stroll back to the inn.

The White Lion

A large country inn dating back to about 1700, the White Lion is opposite the village church. This close affinity led to a local custom whereby newly-married couples were held back at the church gate by a rope, and had to pay a forfeit which was used to good effect by guests and locals who then drank their health in the adjacent inn! Internally the inn has many alcoves and there is a wealth of exposed beams. Food is available every day at lunchtime and during the evening and visitors can choose between a separate restaurant or bar meals. It is worth noting that the inn provides a roast meal every day of the week. Apart from traditional offerings there is an extensive range of 'specials' to tempt the palate. Outside, there is a beer garden and a patio area as well as a play area for children. Telephone: 01928 722949.

The Walk

① On leaving the inn turn right along the roadside pavement. After ¼ mile keep on, past Towers Lane, which goes off to the right. About 250 yards further on, arrive at a track on the right just before dwellings are reached. A sign here indicates Pye Corner Farm.

② Enter the track. Pass dwellings and walk to the side of a facing gate to follow a grassy track which gradually descends. On reaching the bottom of the descent keep forward and climb along a track by a field edge. Arrive at the field corner.

③ Turn left now and then follow the edge of a field which passes close to a tall power pylon. Keep the hedge at the edge of the field on your immediate left. After 2 yards the path gradually bears away from the hedge on the left, until, about ¼ m after passing the pylon, there is a verti wooden footpath signpost.

④ Turn right here (in the direction of t Longster Trail) and pass between bush and gorse to emerge into a large, slopi field. Turn left and follow a path whi gradually descends along the field ed where there are trees on the immediate le Where the trees finish, go over a footbric which takes you over a stream, and follo facing path which leads up a field. Go o a stile at the side of a gate and follo facing track which dips and climbs acr the next field. On reaching the end of field bear right and go over a stile at side of a gate to join a track.

⑤ Turn right along the track. When

field path near Alvanley

ack forks bear right to continue along a
avel track where there are trees on the left
d a field on the right. A little further on
ere is an outbuilding on the left. Keep
rward here to arrive at a gate on the right
here there is a yellow directional arrow.
o through this gate and follow a grassy
ack. The track, which is hedged-in,
adually descends and leads to a fence-
le at the side of a facing gate.

) Cross the fence-stile to enter a large field.
llow the right hand side of the field,
eping a row of trees on your immediate
ht. On nearing the end of the field, bear
t to keep along the top of a banking to
ere, after about 80 yards, there is a path
ich descends to a stile and footbridge in
shes. Cross the footbridge and turn right to
mb to a stile at the end of an outbuilding.
oss the stile and turn left to follow a track
ween outbuildings and a farmhouse.

Follow the track away from the farm, pass a
bungalow, and arrive at a crossing lane.

⑦ Turn right and gradually climb along the
lane. After ½ mile arrive at a crossing road.

⑧ Turn left and follow the roadside
pavement back into Alvanley.

PLACES OF INTEREST NEARBY

The Mouldsworth Motor Museum is about 2½
miles from Alvanley and is reached along minor
roads which connect with the B5393 between
Mouldsworth and Ashton (follow the signs). The
museum is a mecca for anyone with an interest in
the history of transport. There are examples of
early motor cars, Dinky toys, old tools, magazines
and signs from a bygone age together with a
reconstruction of a 1920s garage which really
captures the ambience of an era long since gone.
Telephone: 01928 731781.

Peover Heath
The Dog Inn

MAP: OS LANDRANGER 118 (GR 793736)   **WALK 12**   **DISTANCE:** 2½ MILES

DIRECTIONS TO START: PEOVER HEATH IS ABOUT 1½ MILES FROM THE A50, A535 AND A537 ROADS; FROM THE A50, 2½ MILES TO THE SOUTH OF KNUTSFORD, IT CAN BE REACHED ALONG A LANE WHICH COMMENCES AT THE SIDE OF THE WHIPPING STOCKS INN. **PARKING:** IN THE PUB CAR PARK, WITH PERMISSION.

Old maps reveal that there are a number of 'Peovers' to the south of Knutsford: Lower Peover, Peover Superior and Inferior, Nether Peover and Peover Heath. The name 'Peover' (pronounced Peever) is an ancient one and derives from the Anglo-Saxon 'peefer' – bright river – which refers to a stream called Peover Eye which meanders through the district. The area is one that has changed little over the centuries, where ancient woodlan and old estates are mixed into a most appealir landscape. The walk takes you away fro Peover Heath along a lane prior to crossii lush green fields in a northerly direction. virtually straight cross-country path then lea to a lane for the return stroll back to Peov Heath.

The Dog Inn

The inn, which has been known by several different names over the past 100 years, is very attractive. Internally there are a number of different rooms, a smoke-free dining area where children are most welcome, and various alcoves. A wide range of liquid refreshment is on offer with real ale from Jennings, Greenalls, Flowers and Tetley, as well as a choice of ciders and soft drinks. The inn has built up a reputation for providing excellent value, and, if a meal is required, it is advisable to book in advance although bar snacks are available without booking. Because the choices are varied daily, and to suit each changing season, there is not a set menu. Lunch is served every day between 12 noon and 2.30 pm, and dinner between 7 pm and 9.30 pm. There is a beer garden, and overnight accommodation is also available if required. Telephone: 01625 861421.

The Walk

) On leaving the inn, turn left and follow the lane past a row of terraced houses. About 60 yards after passing a telephone kiosk, the lane turns sharply to the right. Leave the lane here, and pass through a facing gate to follow a macadam drive between tall conifer trees. The drive leads towards Sycamore Farm. Go through a small gate on the right which is close by the entrance gate to the farm and follow a edge which skirts around the farm.

) Where the hedge on the left finishes, turn left and cross a field to go over a double stile which is set between trees. Continue, in the same general direction as before, and then go over a stile in a crossing fence. Bear slightly right now and walk across a field corner to go over a stile which is set in a fence to the left of a large dwelling. Follow a straight macadam drive past dwellings and, after about 300 yards, arrive at a crossing lane.

③ Turn right along the lane. After only 60 yards leave the lane to the left and then turn left again to go through a small wooden gate which gives access to a narrow

PLACES OF INTEREST NEARBY

A little over 1 mile from Peover Heath, and reached by turning left at the crossroads just before Ye Olde Park Gate Inn is reached, is **Peover Hall and Gardens**. Dating from 1585, the hall is well known for its fine Jacobean stables, chapel, landscaped gardens and topiary work. Open from April to October inclusive, hall, gardens and stables are open every Monday, excluding bank holidays, from 2 pm to 5 pm – when there are tours of the hall at 2.30 pm and 3.30 pm. The gardens and stables are also open every Thursday afternoon between 2 pm and 5 pm. Cream teas are available on Monday afternoons. Telephone: 01565 632358.

A waymarked stile near Peover Heath

hedged-in path where there is a tall conifer hedge on the immediate right. Where the hedge on the right finishes, go over a stile to enter a field. Keep along the field edge where, over to the right, about ½ mile away, can be seen a tall water tower – which is a well-known landmark in the area. Pass over a stile at the field corner and follow a well-defined path through scrubland. The path leads to a crossing drive.

④ Walk straight across the drive and keep along a field edge, where there is a fence, interspersed with large trees, on th immediate left. After ½ mile, go over a sti at the side of a gate and arrive at a crossir lane.

⑤ Turn left and follow the lanesic pavement. Pass (or call in – if desired) Y Olde Park Gate Inn. Keep forward at th next junction, in the direction of Peov Heath. Keep on, past a minor lane whic goes off to the right and shortly aft passing Cinder Lane arrive back at the D Inn.

Shotwick
The Yacht Inn

DIRECTIONS TO START: THE YACHT INN FRONTS ONTO THE A540 CHESTER TO HOYLAKE ROAD AT WOODBANK, WHICH IS 5 MILES FROM CHESTER. **PARKING:** IN THE PUB CAR PARK, WITH PERMISSION. ALTERNATIVELY, THERE ARE A COUPLE OF ROADSIDE LAYBYS NEARBY.

For many centuries the village of Shotwick was an important point for travellers journeying to Wales and beyond. A ford and ferry lay close to the village, and these were in constant use prior to the silting up of the Dee Estuary. Today the village lies at the end of a narrow lane, only ½ mile from a busy main road, but nevertheless one still feels miles away from the hurly-burly of modern life when visiting it. Today's walk is a simple one. The outward leg is along an attractive tree-lined lane which leads straight to the village of Shotwick with its quaint houses and interesting church. The return journey utilises a cross-country path which links up with another pleasant country lane on the way back to the Yacht Inn.

43

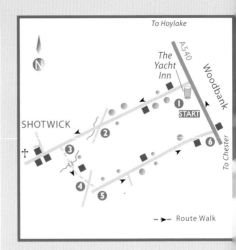

The Yacht Inn

Many years ago, when nearby Shotwick was a port, the Yacht Inn was a favourite with sailors who would walk from the village to quench their thirsts. These sailors of long ago would be pleasantly surprised at the wide range of food and drink to be found at the inn today. There are a number of different beers on offer together with an assortment of lagers, ciders and soft drinks. Being a Millers Kitchen, there is a comprehensive choice of meals to suit every taste, served every day at lunchtime and during the evening, and every Sunday there is a traditional roast lunch. A children's menu is also available. Internally there is a bright ambience provided by the large bay windows of this listed building. Outside there is a large beer garden with a separate play area for children. Telephone: 01244 880216.

The Walk

① Enter Shotwick Lane, which begins at the side of the inn. Follow this delightful lane, with its attractive laneside dwellings half-hidden in trees, for 1 mile, to arrive at a crossing road.

② Cross the road, taking care, and continue along Shotwick Lane. The lane bridges Shotwick Brook now. About ¼ mile further on, keep an eye open for the commencement of a footpath which is the key to your route for the return journey. About 40 yards before arriving at a sign telling you that you are entering Shotwick Village – there are also 30 mph signs here – there is a path up an embankment on the left which leads to a wooden kissing gate.

Make a mental note of where this footpat commences and continue into the village.

The village is only small but is full c character – with stone cottages from bygone age sitting in the shadow of th church of St Michael. There has been church in Shotwick since before the time c the Domesday Book and today it is hard t imagine that the waters of the Dee Estuar once lapped against the sandstone wall o the far side of the church confines. Dow an adjoining lane opposite Stone Cottage Shotwick Hall, now a farm, which is typical gabled house of the 17th century.

Having absorbed the delights of tl village, return along Shotwick Lane to tl point where the previously mentione footpath commences.

③ Leave the lane, climb up a bank and through a kissing gate to enter a slopir field. Descend, and go over a footbrid which takes you over Shotwick Broc Climb up a field, bearing slightly left ar pass through a metal kissing gate which at the side of a field gate. Turn right ar after a few strides pass through anoth gate. Bear left now and cross a field. C

Picturesque cottages in Shotwick

...aching the far side of the field go through ...metal kissing gate which is at the side of ...field gate to arrive at a crossing road.

) Cross the road, taking care, and go over ...stile on the opposite side. Follow a path ...hich cuts across the end of a rough field ...d then pass through bushes and trees. ...he path descends into a gully and then ...merges at a crossing lane.

) Turn left along the lane. Keep on, past ...long, straight, narrow lane which goes off ...the right. Follow the lane for almost a ...le further, passing various dwellings en- ...ute. Shortly after passing The Willows, ...rive at a crossing road.

⑥ Cross the road, taking care, and turn left to follow the roadside pavement. The Yacht Inn soon comes into view straight ahead. Cross the road again, taking care, and arrive back at the inn.

PLACES OF INTEREST NEARBY

Less than 6 miles from the Yacht Inn, and reached via the A540 towards Chester and then the A5117 and A5032 roads, is the **Boat Museum** at Ellesmere Port. The museum is set within a historic dock complex and contains the world's largest floating collection of canal craft. There are indoor exhibitions, a shop and a café and boat trips can be arranged. Telephone: 0151 3555017.

Norley
The Tiger's Head

MAP: OS LANDRANGER 117 (GR 571726) **WALK 14** **DISTANCE:** 3¼ MILES

DIRECTIONS TO START: LEAVE THE A556 BETWEEN SANDIWAY AND DELAMERE TO DRIVE ALONG STONEYFORD LANE IN THE DIRECTION OF NORLEY (1¾) AND KINGSLEY (4). KEEP STRAIGHT AHEAD AND IN ONE MILE ENTER THE FACING COW LANE. AT THE NEXT JUNCTION TURN LEFT, AND THEN LEFT AGAIN, TO ENTER SCHOOL BANK – WHERE THE TIGER'S HEAD IS ON THE RIGHT. **PARKING:** IN THE PUB CAR PARK, WITH PERMISSION. ALTERNATIVELY, LEAVE THE A556 AT DELAMERE AND DRIVE ALONG THE B5152 TOWARDS FRODSHAM TO ARRIVE AT A LARGE PUBLIC CAR PARK AT HATCHMERE WHICH IS OPPOSITE THE CARRIERS INN (START THE WALK AT POINT 5).

In years gone by, Norley was at the centre of the vast expanse of Delamere Forest. In fact, its very name Norley, or Northley as it was once called, means 'north clearing in the forest'. Although much of the forest has long been cleared, the surrounding area is criss-crossed by quiet lanes and paths – which present the enquiring visitor with a means of exploring this lovely area in some detail. From the inn, the route follows lanes and paths to [a] ridge, where there are long views across th[e] valley of the river Weaver. The return leg pass[es] close to Hatchmere – with its attractive reed[-] fringed pool – before returning to Norley alo[ng] lanes, paths and tracks.

The Tiger's Head

An extremely attractive inn which dates back to 1729, the Tiger's Head provides a varied selection of Burtonwood ales and tasty, traditional home-cooked bar meals. During the winter months, two roaring log fires provide a warming glow, whilst in summertime there is an adjacent bowling green which can be utilised (by arrangement). Open every day of the week for liquid refreshment, meals are served every lunchtime and during the evenings – except on Mondays – which is chef's day off. The inn has a children's play area, a function room and can provide overnight accommodation if required. Telephone: 01928 788309.

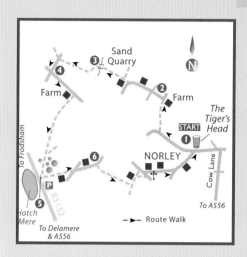

The Walk

) On leaving the inn turn right and adually descend along a narrow hedged-lane. Gradually climb and then go over a ile on the right which is at the side of a eld gate (if you arrive at Damson Cottage ou have gone 30 yards too far). Follow a eld edge, keeping a hedgerow on your imediate left. A farm comes into view raight ahead. Continue along the field ge and then go over three stiles which are at the side of gates close to the farm tbuildings. Emerge at a bend in a ossing lane.

) Turn left and arrive at a crossroads. ep forward here, to enter Town Farm ne. Keep on, past Town Farm and The ddock. Shortly, the lane turns to the left t keep forward here to enter a track at e side of the entrance to a dwelling called e Oranges. Almost immediately there is unction. Keep straight ahead here and

shortly pass a dwelling which is on the right. The route leads along the edge of a huge sand quarry. Gradually descend and pass over a stile. Go straight over a crossing track and descend, to go over a footbridge and stile at the bottom of the descent.

③ Bear left at first, and climb, keeping a fence on your immediate left, and then climb up the facing hillside to follow a grassy area between sandy dirt-tracks. Pass over the track near the top of the climb and keep on along level terrain where there are long views across to the valley of the river Weaver on the right. Go over a stile in a crossing fence and keep on across the next field in the same general direction as before. A stile at the side of a gate gives access to a lane, where the way is left. After 100 yards arrive at a crossroads.

④ Turn left and cross the road, taking care, to follow the roadside grass verge. After 300 yards, and immediately after passing a farm on the right, turn right to walk across a concreted area along the edge of outbuildings. Go through a facing gate and follow a track which leads away from

47

Hatchmere

the farm. The track goes across fields. Pass through a gate – after which the way has become a narrow fenced-in path. Emerge from the path onto a gravel track by a dwelling. Keep forward here, in the same direction as before, to follow the track through trees. Arrive at a junction of paths where the gravel track turns sharply to the right. (The pool at Hatchmere can be seen from here – and this is the joining point if you have parked at that location.)

⑤ Leave the track to the left where a sign points to School Lane. Keep to the right and follow a well-defined path through trees. Join a drive from Flaxmere House and keep forward where a track goes off to the left, to arrive at a road junction. Keep right here, along Post Office Lane. About 100 yards after the pavement ends, arrive at a path on the right.

⑥ Enter the path – which is narrow and hedged-in. Pass through a gate. The path follows a field edge and leads, via a gate, ▸ a crossing track. Turn left. Keep forwar where the track forks to very gradual climb between hedgerows. The track lea to a crossing road. Walk straight across th road, taking care, and turn right. Turn le now to enter Maddocks Hill – whic commences at the side of the Method church. Pass dwellings and, on reaching th next junction, turn left and cross the roa Follow the pavement along School Ba and back to the Tiger's Head.

PLACES OF INTEREST NEARBY

The centre of the largest surviving tract **Delamere Forest** is only a couple of miles to th south-west of Norley – where the now disuse Delamere station of Linmere is the focus for display centre and adjacent picnic sites. Th station is just over one mile north along th B5152 from its intersection with the A556.

Gurnett
The Olde King's Head

DIRECTIONS TO START: GURNETT IS JUST OVER ONE MILE TO THE SOUTH-EAST OF MACCLESFIELD, CLOSE TO THE A523 LEEK ROAD. LEAVE THE A523 WHERE A SIGN POINTS TOWARDS LANGLEY AND WINCLE AND DRIVE ALONG BYRONS LANE. AFTER ½ MILE ARRIVE AT THE HAMLET OF GURNETT. **PARKING:** BECAUSE THE PUB ONLY HAS A TINY CAR PARK, THE LANDLORD HAS REQUESTED THAT WALKERS LEAVE THEIR VEHICLES ON BULLOCKS LANE – ON THE LEFT HAND SIDE, CLOSE TO WHERE THE LANE BRIDGES THE CANAL. ALTERNATIVELY, PARK AT THE HEAD OF SUTTON RESERVOIR. TO REACH THIS PARKING LOCATION, CONTINUE ALONG BULLOCKS LANE AND KEEP FORWARD AT THE CROSSROADS INTO LEEK OLD ROAD; AFTER A FURTHER ½ MILE, YOU COME TO SUTTON RESERVOIR (START THE WALK AT POINT 3).

As well as the magnificent scenery of the green hills of the Peak District National Park, there is a distinctive watery flavour to this walk for, apart from a 2 mile stroll along the towpath of the Macclesfield Canal, the route also passes by the elevated waters of Sutton Reservoir. The initial route goes, via lane and field paths, to the reservoir, followed by a gentle descent along a winding lane to the Fool's Nook Inn prior to the return leg along the canal towpath. There are superb views from the canal towpath across to Tegg's Nose Country Park and the tree-covered hills around Macclesfield Forest.

The Olde King's Head

An established coaching house and smithy since 1695, the Olde King's Head has been of great benefit to travellers by both road and canal over many long years. Having an attractive interior, the pub building dates back to 1627 and is well known for its warm welcome and friendly atmosphere. This is a free house and there is a wide selection of beers and wine from which to choose. Home cooking is the order of the day here and an extensive menu is offered including a traditional Sunday lunch. The pub boasts two double en-suite bedrooms and makes a perfect base from which to explore the local countryside. Open seven days, meals are served Monday to Friday from 11.30 am to 2.30 pm and from 7 pm to 9 pm. On Saturday and Sunday the pub is open all day with meals being served from 12 noon to 2.30 pm and 7 pm to 9 pm. Telephone: 01625 423890.

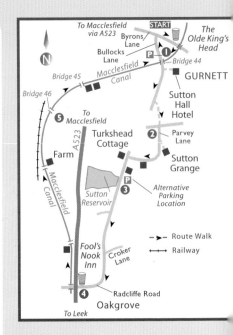

The Walk

① Adjacent to the Olde King's Head there is a cottage called the Old Forge. Ascend steps at the side of the cottage and arrive on the towpath of the Macclesfield Canal. Turn right along the towpath, which shortly forms an aqueduct where it passes over the river Bollin. Just before reaching bridge 44 leave the towpath up broadly spaced steps and turn left to cross over the bridge. Follow a laneside pavement and keep on past the entrance drive of Sutton Hall Hotel. There are dwellings on the right shortly. Leave the lane to the left now, to go over a stile which is opposite a house call Gransden Cottage. You have now entered a large field. Keep ahead for a short

distance and cross a stream which flo~ along a gully. Bear right and, keeping t~ gully on your right, walk towards the rig~ of a three-storey house which can be se~ across the field. On reaching the end of t~ field go over a stile.

② Keep forward, cross a road, and en~ Parvey Lane. Follow the laneside paveme~ and keep on past the entrance drive~ Sutton Grange. The lane bends and, af~ ¼ mile, leads to a T-junction. Turn le~ pass Turkshead Cottage and then ot~ dwellings, to arrive at the head of Sutt~ Reservoir (which is an alternative parki~ location). This is an attractive setting wh~ there is usually a wide variety of aqua~ wildlife to observe.

③ Climb along the facing lane away fr~ the reservoir. Pass a private drive on~ right, which goes to Broadoak Farm, ~ keep on past Croker Lane – which clin~

The Macclesfield canal at Fool's Nook

way to the left. The lane descends shortly and then turns sharply to the right to become Radcliffe Road. A short stroll leads to the busy A523 road close to the Fool's Nook Inn where refreshment can be taken if required.

4 Cross the road, taking care, and go over a swing bridge which takes you over the Macclesfield Canal. Turn right and walk along the canal towpath.

The canal was opened for traffic on 9th November 1831 and connects the Trent and Mersey Canal, near Kidsgrove, with the Peak Forest Canal near Marple. It was originally constructed for the transport of such cargoes as coal, salt, lime and stone, although today it is mostly used by leisure boaters (and, of course, walkers!).

The canal stays parallel to the road, takes you past a cottage and under a footbridge, and then gradually bears away to the left. On passing a swing bridge, which gives access to a farm, the canal runs close to a railway line for a short distance and leads to bridge 46.

5 Keep along the towpath and pass under bridge 46. Continue and, on passing under bridge 45, absorb some superb views ahead towards Tegg's Nose Country Park and the tree-covered hills of Macclesfield Forest. Pass under bridge 44 and leave the canal towpath to the left to arrive back at the car park.

PLACES OF INTEREST NEARBY

The **Silk Museum**, based at the **Heritage Centre** in Macclesfield, relates the fascinating story of the development of silk within the town and shows how important it was to the economy of the area. Open Monday to Saturday, 11 am to 5 pm, Sunday 1 pm to 5 pm. There is a nominal admission charge. Telephone: 01625 617880.

Little Barrow
The Foxcote Inn

MAP: OS LANDRANGER 117 (GR 470699)   **WALK 16**   **DISTANCE:** 2½ MILES

DIRECTIONS TO START: THE B5132 CONNECTS THE A51 AT STAMFORD BRIDGE WITH THE A56 NEAR DUNHAM-ON-THE-HILL. LITTLE BARROW IS SITUATED BETWEEN THESE TWO PLACES WHERE THE FOXCOTE INN IS AT THE TOP OF THE HILL. **PARKING:** IN THE PUB CAR PARK, WITH PERMISSION.

Little Barrow is situated on the gentle slopes of a low sandstone hill about 4 miles from the centre of Chester. There are wonderful views over the surrounding countryside – towards Helsby Hill in the north-east and Beeston and Peckforton in the south-east. There are many attractive old houses in the area, many dating from the 17th and 18th centuries. The village is on the railway line between Chester and Manchester and used to have its own station, which was closed 1953. The walk takes you on a gentle descent a hedged-in path which meanders throu fields before crossing flat agricultural land the banks of the river Gowy. The route pass close to the tiny hamlet of Plemstall, with attractive church – which is well worth a visi prior to returning to Little Barrow along fi paths, tracks and lanes.

The Foxcote Inn

Once called the Railway Inn, due to its close proximity to the Chester to Manchester railway line, this lovely little hostelry is situated at the top of a hill on the edge of the village from where there are extensive views over the surrounding countryside. Once a cottage farmhouse, and over 300 years old, the inn maintains links with its origins by offering traditional farmhouse cooking as well as various seafood specialities of the season. This approach results in an extremely comprehensive, varied and interesting menu with something to tempt every taste. To complement the food there is an extensive range of fine wines as well as the usual beers, lagers, ciders and soft drinks. The inn is open every day with meals being served at lunchtime and during the evenings. Telephone: 01244 301343.

The Walk

) Enter a narrow lane which commences rectly opposite the porch entrance of the n. Gradually descend, between dgerows, and keep on, past a bungalow, arrive at a facing gate near a farm. Go rough the gate and after a couple of ides go over a stile on the left which is at e side of a gate. Follow a hedged-in track. ne track becomes a path between hedge-ws – which can be somewhat overgrown ring high summer. Follow the path as it rns to the right and then to the left near field gate. A grassy track between dgerows leads to a junction of paths.

 Turn right here, where a sign points wards Plemstall. Go over a stile and follow a grassy track for 80 yards and then cross a flat bridge to enter a large field. Walk straight across the field, aiming to the left of a farm which can be seen about 600 yards away. After 250 yards arrive at the banks of the river Gowy, close by a redundant stile.

③ Turn right and follow a riverside path. Go over a stile in a crossing fence and then, 40 yards further on, turn left to cross a bridge which takes you over the river. Bear slightly right now, and walk to the right hand side of a barn, to cross a stile. There is a farm and outbuildings, on the left here. Turn right and follow a track away from the farm. The track passes over the railway; please observe the safety advice and stop, look and listen, before crossing the track. Pass a house which is by the railway line and arrive at a left hand bend in the track.

④ The route is to the right now, away from the track, to pass close to a telegraph pole and then go over a footbridge which traverses the river Gowy. (However, if time allows, it is worth continuing along the track to take a look at Plemstall church.

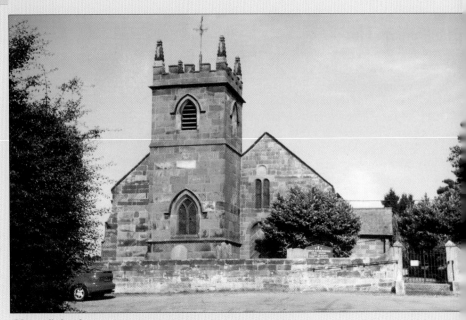

Plemstall church

The main fabric of the church dates from the 15th century and it contains many fine carvings and early printings of the Bible.) Having crossed the footbridge, keep along the left hand edge of a large field, where there are fine views of Helsby Hill straight ahead. On reaching the end of the field go over a wooden footbridge. Walk straight across the next field and go over a stile and plank-bridge.

⑤ Turn right along a well-defined track. The track takes you past a nursery and leads to a crossing lane via a stile.

⑥ Turn right and pass characterf dwellings on a gradual climb back to tl Foxcote Inn.

PLACES OF INTEREST NEARBY

A little over 3 miles by road from Little Barro and reached via the B5132 and A51 via Stamfo Bridge, is the delightful town of **Tarvin**. The tov contains an abundance of Georgian buildings a there is a fine church, which dates back to tl 14th century and houses many interesting relic

Lower Withington
The Red Lion

MAP: OS LANDRANGER 118 (GR 813696) **WALK 17** **DISTANCE:** 3½ MILES

DIRECTIONS TO START: THE B5392 RUNS THROUGH LOWER WITHINGTON ON ITS ROUTE BETWEEN THE A535 AT JODRELL BANK AND THE A34 AT SIDDINGTON. THERE IS A LARGE GREEN HERE, AT THE FAR SIDE OF WHICH IS THE RED LION. **PARKING:** IN THE PUB CAR PARK, WITH PERMISSION.

The village of Lower Withington forms the southern section of the manor of Old Withington, which was acquired about 1266 by a descendent of the Baskervyles who came over from Normandy with Duke William in 1066. The walk heads north into Old Withington along field paths and tracks and then turns west to follow a typical Cheshire lane for a mile before turning south through farms for the return journey to Lower Withington.

The Red Lion

Once a small working farm, the Red Lion stands in 7 acres of prime Cheshire land and for many years it was the venue for the Lower Withington Gooseberry Show. It serves a range of Robinson's ales and provides delicious home-made meals. As well as bar meals there is a large restaurant – both serving the same menu. A particular favourite is the steak, mushroom and claret pie as well as other dishes such as rack of lamb and various steaks. On the lighter side a wide range of sandwiches can be purchased. Open every day for food from 12 noon to 2 pm and 7 pm to 9 pm the inn provides a warm welcome to walkers. During the summer months there is an attractive garden to enjoy. Telephone: 01477 571248.

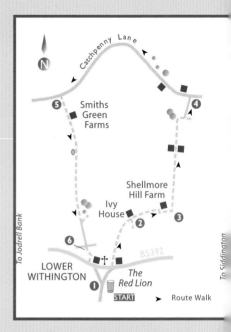

The Walk

① From the Red Lion follow a lane along the right hand side of the village green to arrive at a junction with a crossing road. Turn left and after 80 yards, and before the Methodist chapel is reached, go over a stile on the right where a footpath sign points to Pitt Lane. Keep along the facing field edge and then go over a stile at the side of a field gate. Continue along the edge of the next field and go over a footbridge. The path follows the edge of the next field, where a dwelling can be seen straight ahead. Keep to the right of the dwelling and go over a stile which gives access to a drive which takes you away from the dwelling. The drive leads to a junction at the side of a dwelling called Ivy House.

② Turn left and follow the approach drive to Shellmore Hill Farm. Just before th farmhouse and outbuildings are reache bear to the right to follow a track whic skirts around the outbuildings. The trac follows a field edge where there is hedgerow on the immediate right. Aft 100 yards, there is a junction of tracks.

③ Turn left now, to follow the main trac where there is a hedgerow on the right, a walk in the direction of dwellings whi can be seen about ¼ mile away. Pa through a gate and continue towards t dwellings. Go through two gates in qui succession and walk between the dwelling Go through another two gates a continue along the track which leads aw from the dwellings. After a further 2 yards follow the track as it turns to t right by a nature reserve. About 40 ya further on there is a junction of ways. Tu left now to follow a straight section of la to a junction opposite Ash Tree Cottage

...odrell Bank seen across the fields

...) Turn left to follow a typical, broad-...rged Cheshire lane past a number of ...elightful dwellings. Remain on the lane ...r one mile to where, on the left, you arrive ... the entrance drive of Smiths Green ...arms.

...) Leave the lane and enter the entrance ...ive. Pass a farm which is on the right and ... the second farm walk between the ...rmhouse and outbuildings to join a track ...hich leads away from the farm. Over to ...e right at this point there is a fine view of ...e radio telescope at Jodrell Bank. The ...ck goes past a pond and then skirts the ...ge of a wood. Join a facing macadam lane ...hich leads to a junction near a dwelling.

⑥ Turn left, but after only 20 yards, turn right to follow a narrow path between hedgerows. After 80 yards, a stile gives access to a field. Walk across two small fields and go over two stiles. A narrow fenced-in path between dwellings leads to a crossing road. Turn left and then next right to arrive back at the village green in Lower Withington. A few more strides and you are back at the Red Lion.

PLACES OF INTEREST NEARBY

Only 2 miles from Lower Withington and accessible via the B5392 and A535 road, is the world famous radio telescope at **Jodrell Bank** – where there are space-age exhibitions and a wonderful arboretum to explore. Telephone: 01477 571339.

Wildboarclough
The Crag Inn

DIRECTIONS TO START: WILDBOARCLOUGH IS ABOUT 5 MILES TO THE SOUTH-EAST OF MACCLESFIELD AND IS REACHED ALONG A MINOR ROAD WHICH CONNECTS THE A54 CONGLETON TO BUXTON ROAD WITH THE A537 MACCLESFIELD TO BUXTON ROAD. THE CRAG INN LIES TO THE SOUTH OF THE VILLAGE. **PARKING:** IN THE PUB CAR PARK, WITH PERMISSION. ALTERNATIVELY THERE IS A CAR PARK AND PICNIC SITE AT CLOUGH HOUSE WHICH IS ABOUT 1 MILE TO THE NORTH OF THE CRAG INN (START WALK AT POINT 4).

Wildboarclough is tucked away amongst the lush green folds of the valleys of east Cheshire. This is hilly country, where the effort of climbing is rewarded with magnificent views across the Peak District National Park. It is hard to imagine that around 200 years ago, the area was a hive of industry when the waters of the Clough Brook, which runs through the valley, were harnessed to provide power for the Crag Works – which carried out calico printing From the inn, the route of the walk takes in climb along a narrow lane then joins a trac which meanders along the western side of th valley before dropping down to Clough Hous The return leg is along the opposite side of th valley, passing Crag Hall and graduall descending along lanes, tracks and paths bac to the inn.

The Crag Inn

Situated by the burbling waters of the Clough Brook, this popular inn is at the very heart of a magnificent tract of countryside. Once a farmhouse, the inn exudes character, exemplified by the antique furniture and unusual fittings. A free house, the range of drinks on offer can vary from time to time. Hearty portions of home-cooked food are served every day at lunchtime and during the evening; jacket potatoes and snacks, together with an assortment of sandwiches can also be purchased. Outside, there is an attractive patio area to enjoy when the weather is warm. Conversely, a visit during wintertime is most rewarding when blazing open log fires take away the chill. (Between October and Easter the inn may be closed on Mondays.) Telephone: 01260 227239.

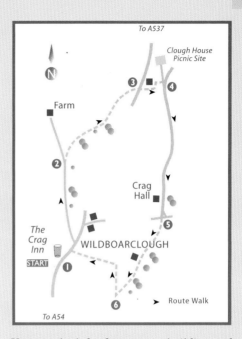

The Walk

① From the inn, turn left and pass the entrance drive to Old Beams Cottage. After 120 yards, fork left and climb up a narrow lane. The lane levels out and is heavily wooded on the right. Arrive at a gate on the right where a sign says Bank Top.

② Go through the gate and follow a gravel track. There is an open, sloping field to the left and a stone wall and trees on the right. Over to the left can be seen the summit of Shutlingsloe, which is almost 1700 feet high. Pass through a gateway, and follow the track as it turns to the right, to a dwelling. There are lovely views across the valley on the right here, to Crag Hall.

Keep to the left of a stone outbuilding and follow a well-defined grassy track, which hugs a stone wall on the left. Cross a stile in a stone wall and descend to go over a stream and a stile. A stile at the side of a gate leads to a crossing lane.

③ Cross the lane and go over a footbridge which takes you over the Clough Brook. Walk straight up the facing field and then turn left and right to pass through the farmyard of Clough House. Emerge from the farmyard through a gate (on the left here, just 100 yards away, is the alternative parking area at Clough House Picnic Site).

④ Having emerged from the farmyard, turn right and almost immediately arrive at a junction where a tree has been planted by the Parish Council. Turn right and gradually climb along a lane. The lane levels out and is a platform for long views in almost every direction. The lane takes

The view near Crag Hall

you past Crag Hall – where there is also a mixture of other dwellings, all tightly inter-mingled. Fork right at the next junction and, after only 30 yards, arrive at a crossing road.

⑤ Cross the road and go over a stone stile at the side of a gate. Follow a gravel track and go through two gates to pass to the rear of a dwelling. Pass through a gateway and follow the track as it winds and then leads past another dwelling. Go through a facing gate and enter an area of open grassland. The path keeps to the slightly higher ground and leads to a footpath marker post which is about 15 yards before a crossing, half derelict, stone wall is reached. This post is about 20 yards away from another wall on the left in front of a tree-lined ridge.

⑥ Turn sharply to the right here and gradually descend to a footbridge, which

can be seen, about 150 yards away. Keep o[n] in the same direction, and after a further [8] yards, cross another footbridge close [to] trees. Follow a path between stone wall[s] and where the wall on the right finishe[s] keep on, to descend to a fence-stile whic[h] can be seen in a stone wall in front of tree[s] straight head. Go over the stile and descen[d] along a rock strewn path. Cross a stur[dy] wooden footbridge to traverse the Cloug[h] Brook once again and turn left for the sh[ort] walk back to the Crag Inn.

PLACES OF INTEREST NEARBY

Less than 3 miles by road from Wildboarcloug[h] and reached by driving to the north from the Cra[g] Inn past Clough House Picnic Site, is **Fore[st] Chapel**, a simple little church erected in 1673 a[nd] rebuilt during 1834. The church is in a picturesq[ue] setting and is well known for its annu[al] Rushbearing Service held on the first Sunday aft[er] 12th August each year.

Marton
The Davenport Arms

MAP: OS LANDRANGER 118 (GR 850682) | **WALK 19** | **DISTANCE:** 4 MILES

DIRECTIONS TO START: THE A34 RUNS NORTH TO SOUTH AND CONNECTS ALDERLEY EDGE WITH CONGLETON. MARTON STRADDLES THIS ROAD 3 MILES FROM CONGLETON. THE DAVENPORT ARMS IS AT THE CENTRE OF THE VILLAGE. **PARKING:** IN THE PUB CAR PARK, WITH PERMISSION. ALTERNATIVELY, THERE IS A VERGESIDE PARKING AREA ON COCKMOSS LANE, WHICH JOINS THE A34 TO THE SOUTH OF MARTON (START WALK AT POINT 6).

This walk, amidst the rolling countryside of south-east Cheshire, presents an opportunity to enjoy long views towards Macclesfield Forest, Shutlingsloe, Croker Hill, Mow Cop and The Cloud. There is also a magnificent timber church to explore – which is quite rightly described as 'one of the ecclesiastical gems of Cheshire'. The initial part of the journey follows a winding lane to a track which takes you past a large trout pool prior to crossing rich farming country for the return to Marton along field paths and lanes.

The Davenport Arms

The inn has an attractive interior with exposed beams and cosy rooms. Bar meals can be purchased and there is also a separate restaurant. Food is served from 12 noon to 2 pm and 6.30 pm to 9.30 pm Tuesday to Saturday and from 12 noon to 2 pm and 7 pm to 9 pm on Sunday. No food is available on Monday. Children are made welcome and there is a pleasant garden to relax in during the summer months. The inn is mentioned in *The Guinness Book of Records* for growing the world's largest gooseberry! Telephone: 01260 224269.

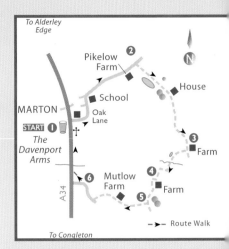

The Walk

① On leaving the inn cross the road, taking care, and turn left to follow the roadside pavement. Turn next right to enter Oak Lane and follow it to a junction near the Primary School. Turn right to follow a lane. After ½ mile, and 150 yards after passing Pikelow Farm, arrive at a track which goes off to the right.

② Enter the track. This takes you close to a large lake which has been developed during recent years into a trout farm. The track passes through a wood and leads past an isolated dwelling. Emerge from the trees and admire long views to Macclesfield Forest, Shutlingsloe, Croker Hill, Mow Cop and The Cloud. Keep along the track and follow it to a farm which sits on higher ground.

③ Walk straight across the farmyard and onto a track. After only 50 yards there is a facing gate. Do not pass through this gate but turn right, to go through an adjacent gate and enter a large sloping field. Kee forward along level ground at first, the descend and pass to the left of a pond converge with a fence on the left. Go ov a gated footbridge which takes you ov Chapel Brook. Keep forward and after yards go over a stile on the right at the si of a field gate. Walk along level groun keeping a fence on your right and turn l at the field corner. Climb towards a far which can be seen on higher ground ahea

④ Go through a kissing gate which is about 25 yards from a hedge in front of t farm. Follow a track to another kissing g and keep along the track which ski around the farm. Pass through a gate a emerge onto a drive where the way is rig Follow the drive away from the farm a pass over a cattle-grid. There is a sm wood of birch trees on the left now. Arr at a cattle-grid where there is a junction ways.

⑤ Do not pass over the cattle-grid, turn right to follow a track. The track le to Mutlow Farm. Go through a gate a bear left between outbuildings. Follow

Marton church

...rive which takes you away from the farm. ...eep on, past the attractive Mosswood ...ottage and arrive at a lane, where the way ...right. The lane turns to right and left in ...ont of an attractive Georgian house. ...here is a footpath sign on the right here – ...nich points to Marton (this is also the ...ternative parking location).

... Leave the lane and pass over a stile ...ich is set in a hedgerow. Bear left and ...nverge with a hedgerow by a row of ...egraph poles. There is a fine view of ...arton church from this path. Go over a ...le at the field corner and turn left. Pass ...se to a building and go through a gate ...ere a short length of drive gives access to ...rossing road. Turn right and follow the ...dside pavement back into Marton.

Before heading home, take a look at one of the finest timber churches in Europe. Founded in 1343, the unusually shaped bell tower and chamber are covered with wooden slates and the whole building has a pleasing exterior. Internally, there are frescos and paintings together with old stone effigies.

PLACES OF INTEREST NEARBY

About 3 miles to the north of Marton, and accessible via the A34, is **Capesthorne Hall, Park and Gardens**. The hall possesses a fascinating collection of paintings, furniture and tapestries whilst the adjoining park, gardens and woodlands extend to some 60 acres. The estate is usually open from the end of March to the end of September on Sundays and Wednesdays and all bank holidays. The gardens are open between 12 noon and 6 pm and the hall between 1.30 pm and 3.30 pm. Telephone: 01625 861221.

Little Budworth
The Egerton Arms

MAP: OS LANDRANGER 117 (GR 594654)   **WALK 20**   **DISTANCE:** 2½ MILES

DIRECTIONS TO START: LITTLE BUDWORTH IS 3 MILES TO THE NORTH-EAST OF TARPORLEY, AND LIES CLOSE TO THE INTERSECTION OF THE A49 AND A54 NEAR OULTON PARK RACING CIRCUIT. THE EGERTON ARMS IS ON PINFOLD LANE TO THE WEST OF THE VILLAGE CENTRE. **PARKING:** IN THE PUB CAR PARK, WITH PERMISSION, ALTERNATIVELY, THERE IS A PUBLIC CAR PARK ON COACH ROAD.

During the Middle Ages, the area around Little Budworth was extensively wooded, being part of the great forests of Mara and Mondrum. Today, the common to the west of the village represents the last remaining trace of these forests in the parish – and the area has been designated a Site of Special Scientific Interest. From the inn, the walk takes you through the centre of the villa before following a path alongside the waters Budworth Pool prior to joining a series cross-country tracks through some attracti countryside. The return leg skirts the edge Little Budworth Common on the way back the Egerton Arms.

The Egerton Arms

A traditional country pub, situated close to Oulton Park Cricket Club, the Egerton Arms is an owner-managed free house of considerable charm. Set well back from Pinfold Lane, its appearance is more that of a country house than an inn. Thwaites Cask Ale is served, together with Double-Diamond, Tetley Bitter, Tetley Smooth, Guinness, draught cider, various lagers and a comprehensive range of soft drinks. The inn also provides delicious snacks including a wide selection of sandwiches, steak 'batches' and a variety of pies – all served with a choice of salads. Food is available every Saturday and Sunday, as well as bank holidays, between 12 noon and 8 pm. During the week the inn is open only during the evenings from 6.30 pm and food is not currently available on weekday evenings. When the weather is warm visitors can relax in an extremely attractive garden where tables and chairs are provided. Telephone: 01829 760250.

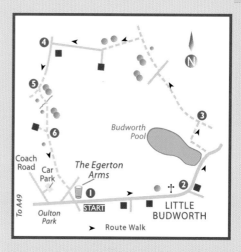

The Walk

On leaving the Egerton Arms turn left, and then left again, to join Vicarage Lane. Follow the laneside pavement and keep on past Booth Avenue to enter the heart of the village. On the left is the parish church of St Peter which was built in 1800 on the site of a much earlier church. Across the lane from the church the Red Lion Inn has for many years been a favourite meeting place for racing drivers from nearby Oulton Park.

Turn left to enter Mill Lane and gradually descend along the laneside pavement. About 50 yards after the pavement terminates go over a stile on the left to follow a path which runs along the edge of Budworth Pool. The path leads to a stile. Go over the stile and walk away from the waterside to cross two small fields via stiles to enter a track.

③ Turn left along the track. Looking back from here, there is a pleasing view across Budworth Pool. The track leads to a crossing lane. Turn right and then immediately left to continue along another, hedged-in track. Arrive at a junction of tracks, where the way is left. On meeting a macadam drive turn right and follow it past Hollybush Bungalow and Hollybush Cottage to arrive at a junction.

④ Turn left. The macadam finishes near dwellings. Keep forward now to follow a facing track which gradually descends. Care is required in order not to miss the route. Having walked along the track for about 150 yards, and 10 yards after passing a field gate on the left, there is a narrow path which goes off to the left.

⑤ Leave the track at this point and follow

A field path near Little Budworth

the path, which descends along a gully. On reaching the bottom of the gully ignore a crossing path and keep forward to follow a track between fences. The track leads over a brook and to the left of a gate before climbing through trees. Emerge onto a broad track close by a private entrance gate.

⑥ Keep forward along a broad, level track. Pass an attractive dwelling and continue to a crossing lane. Turn right here, and then left, to enter Pinfold Lane. At the head of the lane there is an example of a restored 17th century 'pinfold' – an enclosure in which stray animals w⚫ impounded until claimed on payment o⚫ fine. Keep on, past Oulton Park Cric⚫ Club to arrive back at the Egerton Arm⚫

PLACES OF INTEREST NEARBY

Situated by the A49, to the north of the A⚫ junction, is the specialist nursery called Chesh⚫ **Herbs** where all kind of plants and her⚫ products can be admired and purchased. Ther⚫ also an attractive display garden to wan⚫ around. Admission and parking are f⚫ Telephone: 01829 760578.

Brereton Green
The Bear's Head

DIRECTIONS TO START: THE BEAR'S HEAD IS CLOSE BY THE A50 HOLMES CHAPEL TO ALSAGER ROAD AT BRERETON GREEN, 2 MILES TO THE SOUTH OF HOLMES CHAPEL. **PARKING:** IN THE PUB CAR PARK, WITH PERMISSION. THERE IS A CAR PARK NEAR ST OSWALD'S CHURCH (POINT 2) BUT THIS IS FOR VISITORS TO THE CHURCH.

Brereton Green with its handsome 15th century church and fine 16th century hall is a delightful place – where lush green meadows run down to the winding river Croco. The history of the hall and church are closely interwined and it is believed that one of the ancestors of the Brereton family from the nearby hall pledged to build the church in gratitude for his safe return from the Crusades.

The walk takes you close to the hall and past the church before following the course of a track through some attractive countryside. A short stretch of field path then leads onto a lane. The lane meanders through a fertile agricultural area prior to a field path which takes you over the river Croco and back to Brereton church for the short stroll back to the Bear's Head.

The Bear's Head

A former coaching inn with an appealing, ivy-covered façade, the Bear's Head has for many years been the focal point of village social life. Legend has it that Sir William Brereton, who lived in the nearby Brereton Hall, was challenged to design an effective muzzle for a bear! His design was successful and a muzzled bear's head was incorporated into his family emblem – and in turn became the name of the inn. Now quite a large establishment the inn offers, amongst others, Bass and Worthington ales. An extremely wide range of food is also available, with something to suit every taste. Sandwiches, salads, steaks, grills and even six course meals can be purchased. Open every day, food is served between 12 noon and 9.30 pm. There is an attractive beer garden and the inn provides motel accommodation if required. Telephone: 01477 544732.

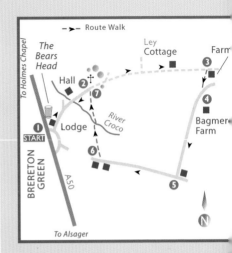

The Walk

① Turn left on leaving the inn and follow the roadside pavement past Smithy Cottage. Turn next left to pass between lodge houses where an arch spans the lane. A sign here indicates the church and hall. Where the lane forks bear right. Shortly, over to the left, there is a fine view across meadows towards Brereton Hall. The hall, which was erected during the 16th century, is one of the finest examples of its kind in Cheshire. The lane bridges the winding river Croco. On the left here, there is a car park for visitors to the adjacent church.

② Pass the impressive entrance gates of Brereton Hall and arrive at the church

entrance gate. The church dates from 11⁹ but was completely rebuilt during the 15 century. Dedicated to St Oswald, contains a monument which sho William Smethwick, who died in 1643. leaflet describing points of interest f visitors is available inside. Continue pε the church along a gravel track. C through a gate at the side of a cattle-gr and then bear right where the track for Keep on through a gate at the side of dwelling. The track takes you past t isolated Ley Cottage. Care is required no in order not to miss the way. About yards before arriving at a tennis court the right and a track which goes off to t left, there is a clump of bushes on the rig

③ Leave the track here, to go over a s which is at the rear of the bushes and en a field. Follow the field edge, keeping fence, interspersed with large trees, on yε immediate left. Walk towards a farm ε then go over a stile in a fence. Keep on the same direction as before, to go o another stile in front of the farm. The fε is called Bagmere Lodge. Arrive or crossing lane.

dge houses near the start of the walk

Turn right along the lane. Keep on past
gmere Farm – which has very attractive
rdens in front of it. Over to the left there
a fine view of Mow Cop on the skyline.
ter ½ mile arrive at a junction of lanes
se by Broad Hay Lodge.

Turn right now where a sign tells you
t Brereton Green is ¾ mile away. Keep
, past a large detached bungalow called
zelbury. About 150 yards after passing
zelbury Farm, and immediately on
ssing house number 56, arrive at a path
ich begins through a gate on the right.

Leave the lane here and go through the
e to enter a large field. The path runs
ng the edge of the field, staying close by
edgerow on the right. After 250 yards,
over a stile in a crossing fence where the
dgerow on the right terminates. Keep
ward, in the same direction as before,

and descend. Go over a footbridge, which
traverses the river Croco, and then walk
across an undulating field in the direction
of St Oswald's church which can be seen,
half-hidden by trees, straight ahead. Cross
a stile opposite the church.

⑦ You are now back on part of your initial
route. Turn left and make your way back to
the Bear's Head.

PLACES OF INTEREST NEARBY
Less than 3 miles from the Bear's Head and
reached by turning right off the A50 along the
A5022 just to the south of Brereton Green, is the
ancient town of **Sandbach**. The main feature of
the town is a delightful cobbled market place
where there are two Anglo-Saxon sandstone
crosses. Apart from the crosses, there are
numerous historic buildings, old inns and
interesting shops to explore.

Church Minshull
The Badger Inn

MAP: OS LANDRANGER 118 (GR 665605)   **WALK 22**   **DISTANCE:** 1¾ MILES

DIRECTIONS TO START: CHURCH MINSHULL STRADDLES THE B5074 BETWEEN WINSFORD AND NANTWICH. THE BADGER INN IS AT THE CENTRE OF THE VILLAGE, NEXT TO THE CHURCH. **PARKING:** THERE IS A PARKING AREA AT THE SIDE OF THE INN AND ADJACENT POST OFFICE (FOR PATRONS OF THE INN).

Church Minshull owes its existence to its strategic location at the point where a spur of the Roman road from Nantwich to Middlewich crossed the river Weaver. The village is rich in half-timbered dwellings, one such being Church Farm on the opposite side of the road from the Badger Inn whose porch juts out towards the road and is supported on pillars. The farm was once the home of Elizabeth Minshull who was married to the 17th century poet John Milton. T village has a smithy and a mill, which, apa from producing flour, provided electricity f the local community up to 1960. The wa follows an attractive country lane and cross the river Weaver before reaching the towpa of the Shropshire Union Canal. A ¾ m stretch along the canal towpath leads to a la for a short stroll back to Church Minshull.

The Badger Inn

A grade II listed building of historic and architectural interest, originally a farmhouse, the Badger Inn has built up an excellent reputation for its food during recent years. Patrons have the option of using restaurant facilities or choosing a bar meal. The range of food is extremely varied from sandwiches, snacks, light meals and salads to full-blown five course meals with all the trimmings. There are also many tempting desserts to choose from as well as a varied wine list. Meals are served at lunchtimes and during the evenings. The inn offers at least five different beers, all served from the cask. There is an attractive beer garden at the rear of the inn close by the church confines. Telephone: 01270 522607.

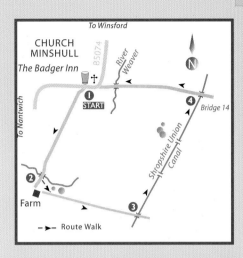

The Walk

① On leaving the main entrance of the inn cross the road, turn right, and then left to enter a lane between dwellings. A sign close to the start of this lane says 'Church Fields'. A narrow hedged-in lane takes you across fields and away from the village. Arrive at a bridge which carries the lane across a river and towards a farm.

The river is the Weaver which is Cheshire's premier natural waterway, for the whole of its 53 mile course is within the boundary of the county. It rises in the Peckforton Hills, flows south at first towards Audlem, then turns north and passes through Nantwich, Winsford and Northwich to enter the Mersey near Frodsham.

② Immediately on crossing the bridge go over a stile on the left. Climb along a path which takes you away from the river and then pass over a stile at the side of a gate. Turn left now to gradually climb along a drive which leads away from the farm. Arrive at a bridge which carries the drive over a canal.

③ Do not cross the bridge but leave the drive to the left and descend steps onto the towpath of the canal. Turn left and follow the towpath away from the bridge.

You are now walking alongside the Middlewich Branch of the Shropshire Union Canal. Affectionately known as the 'Shroppie', the canal links Ellesmere Port with Wolverhampton, where it joins the Staffordshire and Worcestershire Canal. From Ellesmere Port, the canal passes through Chester – where there is a connection with the river Dee, after which it goes through Nantwich and Audlem – at which point it enters Shropshire. The canal has two important branch lines which are less than 2 miles apart to the north of Nantwich. One of these branches goes to Llangollen, the other – which you are now walking along – goes to Middlewich.

Pass under bridge number 12 and

The river Weaver

continue along the towpath. Shortly, over to the left, there is a fine view across fields to Church Minshull. Pass under the next bridge and continue to bridge number 14.

The route is up steps at the side of bridge 14 to pass through a gate which gives access to a road. However, you may wish to extend the walk by continuing along the canalside for as far as you desire and then returning to bridge 14.

④ Turn left along the road and walk away from the bridge to pass the entrance drive of Higher Elms Farm. Descend, and the follow a roadside pavement. The roa bridges the river Weaver and leads ba into Church Minshull village and t Badger Inn.

PLACES OF INTEREST NEARBY

Less than 6 miles to the south of Church Minshu and accessible via the B5074 and A51 road, is t interesting old market town of **Nantwich**, whi is famous for its fine half-timbered buildings a beautiful church.

Brookhouse Green
The Bull's Head

MAP: OS LANDRANGER 118 (GR 799598)	**WALK 23**	DISTANCE: 3½ MILES

DIRECTIONS TO START: THE BULL'S HEAD SITS AT THE SIDE OF THE A50 HOLMES CHAPEL TO ALSAGER ROAD NEAR SMALLWOOD, 5 MILES TO THE SOUTH OF HOLMES CHAPEL. **PARKING:** IN THE PUB CAR PARK, WITH PERMISSION.

The tiny hamlet of Brookhouse Green is at the heart of an area which has for the past two centuries provided the Potteries with much of its fresh vegetables. For all this industry, the area possesses a quiet charm, where a stroll across its fields and along its lanes takes you through a landscape which has changed little during living memory. From the Bull's Head to the turning point at Brookhouse Green, the walk follows a long field path which goes through Overton Green. Country lanes then lead to Smallwood – after which Overton Green is revisited prior to the final leg across field paths.

73

The Bull's Head

You can be assured of a warm welcome at this impressive roadside hostelry. Low beams abound, and during wintertime real fires add a homely touch. Originally a coaching inn, the premises were turned into a blacksmith's workshop for a number of years before reverting back to the provision of food and drink. Ale is provided by Tetley and there is a guest ale which changes every month. Food is served every day both at lunchtime and during the evening. Good quality, old-fashioned, English style meals are the order of the day here with hearty portions at sensible prices. Light snacks can also be purchased. Although food can be consumed anywhere throughout the pub there is a separate non-smoking dining room. The pub has an award-winning beer garden, two conservatories and a children's play area. Telephone: 01477 500247.

The Walk

① On leaving the Bull's Head turn left and follow the roadside pavement to the adjacent traffic lights. Turn left, in the direction of Smallwood, and after 80 yards go over a stile which is set in a hedgerow on the left. Bear slightly right and cross a large field. After 250 yards go over a stile in a crossing hedgerow and continue across the next field. After a further 250 yards go over another stile in a crossing hedgerow. Across to the left can be seen a red brick farmhouse, but keep straight ahead to gradually converge with a hedgerow on the right. Keeping the hedgerow on your immediate right pass between posts and go over a stile. Follow a field edge and go over

a stile at the field corner. Descend step onto a crossing lane.

② Turn left and pass the entrances t Overton Green Farm and Old Farm. Th is the tiny hamlet of Overton Green Immediately on passing Old Farm tur right to follow a track. After 80 yard follow the track as it turns to the righ After only a further 30 yards arrive at junction of paths. Turn left here and wa across a large field in the direction of tre which can be seen about ¼ mile awa Gradually converge with a fence on the le and then cross a stile at the side of a fie gap. Continue, in the same direction before, keeping the fence on you immediate right. The fence terminates at hedgerow. Follow the hedgerow and whe it turns to the right keep forward, stayi parallel with trees on the right. reaching the end of the field go over a st by a brook. Pass over the brook via

wide path near Overton Green

mile and pass various dwellings en-route.

④ Pools Lane terminates at a crossing road. Walk straight over the road to enter a hedged-in path. After 300 yards arrive at a junction. Turn right now to follow a hedged-in track. Keep on past Deers Green Farm. The way has a macadam surface now and takes you past another farm. Arrive at a crossroads.

⑤ Turn left and after 250 yards arrive at a junction in the village of Smallwood. Turn right here, to enter School Lane. Pass the church and village school and keep on past a lane which goes off to the right. A red brick dwelling comes into view ahead. Keep an eye open for steps and a stile on your left. (If you arrive at the entrance to Overton Green Farm you have gone 80 yards too far.)

⑥ Climb up the steps and go over the stile. You are now back on part of the initial route. The facing field path leads back to the road near the crossroads close by the Bull's Head. Turn right here – where a few more strides take you back to the car park.

arth-topped bridge and follow a well-efined path through trees to turn right ong a field edge. After only 50 yards bear ght to enter trees. Turn left now and llow a path through the trees and past lf-hidden ponds. A tree-lined path leads a crossing lane.

) Turn right along the lane. Pass the tractive Cranberry and Chantry Cottages d arrive at a junction close to the lethodist church. This is the sleepy mlet of Brookhouse Green. The way is raight ahead in the direction of Spen reen, Brownlow and Smallwood. About yards further on, and by the entrance to me Tree Farm, bear right to descend ong Pools Lane. Follow the lane for ½

PLACES OF INTEREST NEARBY

About 2 miles from the Bull's Head, and reached by turning right at the adjacent traffic lights and then crossing the A533, is **The Potters Barn** at Hassall Green. This is a traditional working pottery where handmade gifts for house and garden can be purchased. Admission is free and the pottery is open all year. Telephone: 01270 884080.

Aldford
The Grosvenor Arms

DIRECTIONS TO START: THE GROSVENOR ARMS SITS AT THE SIDE OF THE B5130 IN THE VILLAGE OF ALDFORD, MIDWAY BETWEEN CHESTER AND FARNDON. **PARKING:** IN THE PUB CAR PARK, WITH PERMISSION. ALTERNATIVELY, THERE IS A VILLAGE CAR PARK ON CHURCH LANE (SEE POINT 6).

As its name suggests, Aldford was at an old fording point on the nearby river Dee. Most of the village and the surrounding countryside is owned by the Duke of Westminster whose home, Eaton Hall, is just over 1 mile away. The village architecture is also very distinctive with similar bricks, low-pitched roofs and diamond-leaded windows to be seen in abundance. On leaving the village, the walk follows a track which gently descends to the banks of the river Dee. A riverside path then leads to a most appealing bridge of intricate ironwork after which the route cuts through part of the Eaton Estate. Field paths then take you past the remains of a motte and bailey castle to Aldford church. The final leg of the stroll is through the heart of the village on the way back to the Grosvenor Arms.

The Grosvenor Arms

Built in the style of the surrounding village houses, the inn has been developed during recent years into an establishment of taste and charm. There is a main room containing a library, a bar area, a tap room – where a roaring fire provides warmth during cooler weather – and a conservatory. All four rooms, which are interlinked, can be utilised for the enjoyment of food and drink. Being a free house, there are always at least five different beers on offer as well as a selection of wines and over one hundred malt whiskies! The choice of food is extremely wide-ranging, with the menu being changed weekly. There is a choice of six starters, over a dozen main courses, and a selection of sweets. Ploughman's lunches, snacks and various sandwiches can also be purchased. The inn is open every day between 11.30 am and 11 pm with food being served from 12 noon to 10 pm (9 pm on Sundays). During the summertime there is a large beer garden and adjacent terrace to enjoy. Telephone: 01244 620228.

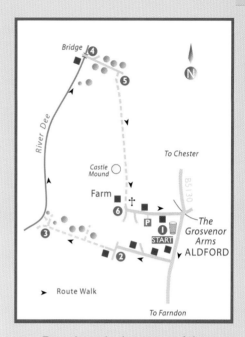

The Walk

1) On leaving the inn turn right and follow the roadside pavement. Pass Bank Farm and other dwellings, many of which have been converted into small businesses during recent years. Immediately on passing The Gables, turn right to enter Green Lake Lane. Keep on, past Middle Lane, which goes off to the right, and arrive at a junction with School Lane.

2) Turn left. After only 30 yards turn right follow a short length of lane to a facing gate. Pass through the gate and keep on along a hedged-in track. After 120 yards there is a track which goes off to the right – but ignore this and very gradually descend along the facing track. After a further 150 yards, and just before it turns to the left, the track levels out. There are two field gaps on the left here.

3) Leave the track now and enter trees on the right. A facing path leads to a gate which is about 30 yards away, but bear left to where after 50 yards, you reach the edge of the river Dee. Turn right and almost immediately go over a stile. Follow a path which stays close to the river and at times meanders along the edge of a very large field where there is a farm and glimpses of the spire of Aldford church over to the right. After about ½ mile, a bridge and boat house come into view. Pass through a gate and follow a path through trees to arrive at the bridge. This most elegant structure was

The river Dee at Chester

built during 1824 to provide access to Eaton Hall – which is on the other side of the river.

④ Do not cross the bridge but follow a macadam drive away from it. Almost immediately there is a fork. Bear right here and follow the drive through a most attractive parkland setting where there are trees on both sides. Where the trees on the right finish, Aldford church comes into view across fields over to the right.

⑤ Leave the drive and turn right to go through a gate which gives access to a field. A well-worn path leads across the field towards the church. Pass through a kissing gate which is set in a crossing fence. The path leads to a gate at the right of the church.

⑥ Pass through the gate and follow the perimeter of the church confines. Turn ne[xt] left and pass the main entrance of th[e] church – opposite which is Middle La[ne] and the village post office. Keep on past th[e] telephone kiosk (on the right is the villa[ge] car park – which is the alternative parki[ng] location). Arrive at a junction close [to] ornate entrance gates which give access [to] Eaton Hall and turn right for the sho[rt] stroll back to the Grosvenor Arms.

PLACES OF INTEREST NEARBY

Less than 5 miles to the north of Aldford, a[nd] reached via the B5130, is the historic city [of] **Chester**. The city has a rich architectural herita[ge] where a mixture of 17th century dwellings, wi[th] mainly Victorian black and white facades, ble[nd] with stately Georgian houses. There is a[n] imposing cathedral, traces of Roman occupatio[n,] a virtually complete circuit of city walls a[nd] pleasure craft for hire on the river Dee.

Bunbury
The Dysart Arms

MAP: OS LANDRANGER 117 (GR 568582) | **WALK 25** | DISTANCE: 2 MILES

DIRECTIONS TO START: BUNBURY LIES LESS THAN A MILE TO THE EAST OF THE A49
TARPORLEY TO WHITCHURCH ROAD, 3 MILES TO THE SOUTH OF TARPORLEY. THE DYSART
ARMS IS IN THE SHADOW OF THE ANCIENT CHURCH. **PARKING:** IN THE PUB CAR PARK,
WITH PERMISSION. ALTERNATIVELY, THERE IS A PARKING LAYBY ON THE OPPOSITE SIDE
OF THE CHURCH FROM THE INN.

The ancient village of Bunbury lies in rich farming country close to the Central Cheshire Sandstone Ridge. The settlement, which has a long history, is mentioned in the Domesday Book. There are numerous black and white half-timbered cottages and other interesting buildings to interest the inquiring visitor. However, pride of place must go to its beautiful church, which sits on a rise and dominates the surrounding landscape. Dedicated to St Boniface, who became the Apostle of Germany and who died in AD 755, the church contains the alabaster tomb and effigy of Sir Hugh Calveley, a distinguished soldier who died in 1394. The walk begins in the shadow of the church and then leads across fields to join up with a quiet country lane for the return to Bunbury. On reaching the outskirts of the village another field path is utilised on the way back to the inn.

The Dysart Arms

Built over 200 years ago and originally a farmhouse, the inn has had a chequered history. At one time it was owned by the influential Tollemache family who, amongst other enterprises, constructed Peckforton Castle. Converted into licensed premises some time after 1850, the establishment that we see today is an attractive village inn where food and drink can be enjoyed in comfort. Being a free house, the liquid refreshment is liable to change from time to time. Delicious home-cooked food is the order of the day here with speciality dishes such as duck and salmon being offered as well as more traditional fare. Home-prepared soups, sandwiches and light snacks can also be purchased and there is a wide range of desserts. Opening hours for drinks are Monday to Saturday 11.30 am to 11 pm, Sunday 12 noon to 10.30 pm. Food is available Monday to Friday from 12 noon to 2.15 pm and 6 pm to 9.30 pm, Saturday 12 noon to 9.30 pm and Sunday 12 noon to 9 pm. During the daytime children of all ages are most welcome, however, after 6 pm it is requested that it should be over 10s only. There is an attractive beer garden at the side of the inn and a couple of swings for children to play on. Telephone: 01829 260183.

The Walk

① On leaving the front door of the inn, turn right and then right again, to descend along Vicarage Lane. After 200 yards the lane turns to the left.

② Leave the lane to the right here, through a kissing gate. Follow a well-

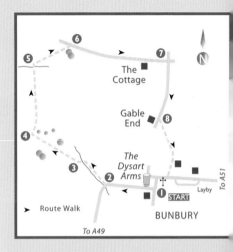

defined track which runs across a field where there is a brook on the left. After 25 yards, bear left at a telegraph pole, cross the brook, and immediately pass over a stile.

③ Turn right and follow a field edge. After 80 yards go over a stile in a crossing fence and keep along a well-defined path which goes through a plantation. Pass over a stile in a crossing hedgerow and gradually climb through the plantation. The path leads to a stile at the side of a row of tall conifer trees.

④ Cross the stile and turn right. After only 15 yards, go over another stile, which is set in a hedgerow, and enter a large field. With the stile at your back, walk straight across the field, aiming to the right of a building which can be seen, in trees, about 1/4 mile away. Gradually descend across the field and, on reaching its far side, go over a stile and cross a sturdy footbridge.

⑤ Bear right now and gradually climb across an undulating field and then go over a stile in a crossing hedgerow, which is to the left of two trees growing in the field. Arrive at a crossing lane.

...ome of the charming cottages in Bunbury

) Turn right along the lane. Keep on, ...st an attractive dwelling called The ...ottage, and arrive at a crossroads.

) Turn right in the direction of Bunbury. ...fter ¼ mile, and just before reaching a ...velling on the right called Gable End, ...rive at a stile which is set in a hedgerow ... the left.

) Go over the stile and enter a field. Bear ...ght and cross the field in the direction of ...uses which are some distance to the left ... the church. On reaching the far side of ... field go over a stile and follow a path along the edge of a graveyard. Emerge from the graveyard over a stile and arrive at a lane opposite the church confines. Turn right and stroll back to the Dysart Arms, which is only a few steps away.

PLACES OF INTEREST NEARBY

About 2 miles to the west of Bunbury, and signed from the A49, is **Beeston Castle**. Built during the early 13th century, the castle played an important role during the Civil War (1642–49). Although now ruinous, the site is an interesting one, and the views from the summit of the crag on which the castle stands are superb.

Brown Knowl
The Copper Mine

DIRECTIONS TO START: ABOUT 10 MILES TO THE SOUTH-EAST OF CHESTER THERE IS A JUNCTION BETWEEN THE A41 AND A534 ROADS AT BROXTON. THE COPPER MINE FRONTS ONTO THE A534 JUST OVER 1 MILE FROM THIS JUNCTION, IN THE DIRECTION OF NANTWICH. **PARKING:** IN THE PUB CAR PARK, WITH PERMISSION.

The village of Brown Knowl is situated on the lower slopes of Bickerton Hill – which was used to advantage by Iron Age man, who built a fortified stronghold close to the cliffs on its north side. If you are feeling energetic there is an opportunity to climb to the top of this hill, otherwise a gentle stroll in and around the village may best suit your mood. Initially, the route follows field paths to a scenic lane which in turn takes you into th[e] village. The Methodist church in the villag[e] centre is a fitting memorial to John Wedgwoo[d] of Potteries fame, who was responsible f[or] bringing Methodism to the area, and was, at h[is] own request, buried in the church confine[s.] From the church, a further mixture of lan[e] circumnavigate the village and lead back to t[he] inn.

The Copper Mine

At the heart of the old copper mining industry which once flourished in the surrounding hills, the Copper Mine is an appealing traditional family-run pub and restaurant. Internally, there is a wealth of brassware and artefacts associated with the mining of copper. A number of intimate, interlinked, open-plan rooms, together with an adjoining conservatory, create a pleasing ambience, where food and drink can be consumed in comfort. Cask ales from Bass and Worthington are served, together with Guinness and an assortment of lagers, ciders and soft drinks. The inn is open from 12 noon to 3 pm and 6 pm to 11 pm (10.30 pm on Sundays) with food being served every day from 12 noon to 3 pm and 6 pm to 9 pm. The range on offer is extensive, with many tempting dishes and bar snacks to choose from. Specialities include spare ribs and delicious home-made steak and kidney pies. The inn welcomes children, for whom there is a separate menu, and a favourite with families is the special roast meal which is available every Sunday. When the weather is fine there is a delightful adjacent beer garden to enjoy. Telephone: 01829 782293.

The Walk

1 On leaving the main roadside entrance to the inn, turn right and follow the verge in the direction of Bickerton. After only 100 yards, go over a stile on the right to enter a field. Keep forward and, on reaching the far side of the field, pass over another stile. A house can be seen straight ahead, about 150 yards away. The path hugs a hedgerow on the right and leads to facing outbuildings where there is a gate and stile to their right. Do not go over this stile.

2 Turn left in front of the stile to walk parallel with a fence. After only 50 yards go over a stile in a crossing fence. After a further 50 yards go over a stile which is set in the fence on the right. Walk between fences now to where, after only 20 yards, there is a stile on the left.

3 Cross the stile to enter a field. Follow the right hand edge of the field and after only 40 yards go over a stile on the right. Walk straight across a field to a stile which can be seen about 90 yards away. Cross the stile to enter a lane.

4 Turn right and follow the lane past Hillside Cottage and other dwellings. At the next junction turn left to enter the village of Brown Knowl. Shortly, on the right, is the rather plain red brick building of the Methodist church. (Across the road from the church, and commencing between dwellings, is a footpath which leads to the top of Bickerton Hill – a climb of about 15 minutes.)

The view seen from the pub

⑤ Follow the lane past the church and keep right at the junction with Lower Sandy Lane. Keep on, past Sandy Lane, and then turn next right to enter Hill Lane. Gradually descend along Hill Lane and arrive at Broomhill Lane, which goes off to the right.

⑥ Enter Broomhill Lane and follow it to the next junction, where the way is left. At the next junction, and opposite the Old Bakery, turn right to enter a lane which takes you back to the Copper Mine.

PLACES OF INTEREST NEARBY

About 2 miles to the north-east of the Copper Mine, and accessible via a lane which commences opposite the inn, is **Cheshire Candle Workshop** at Burwardsley. The hand carving of candles can be observed together with the production of glassware and jewellery. There are extensive showrooms with many crafts and other goods for sale. The workshops are open seven days a week 10 am to 5 pm. Telephone: 01829 770401.

Faddiley
The Thatch Inn

DIRECTIONS TO START: THE THATCH INN SITS AT THE SIDE OF THE A534 ROAD
4 MILES TO THE WEST OF NANTWICH. **PARKING:** IN THE PUB CAR PARK,
WITH PERMISSION.

Although not very well known, Faddiley has had a most chequered history. The village is the reputed site of the Battle Feathanleag which took place in AD 584, during which the Britons, lead by Brochwel, Prince of Powys, defeated Ceawlin, King of the West Saxons. The area is predominantly agricultural and is criss-crossed by a lattice-work of quiet, virtually traffic-free, lanes – which provide an opportunity to stroll through a very lovely tract of Cheshire countryside. The initial stages of the walk are across fields and then along a series of lanes before cutting across country once again to link up with a most delightful lane. The final stage of the route is along an easy to follow field path which crosses an undulating area of countryside on the way back to the inn.

The Thatch Inn

A picturesque gem, the Thatch Inn is the very epitome of an English country hostelry and its beautiful thatched exterior and immaculate front garden have been the subject of countless photographs and paintings. The interior is just as pleasing with oak beams, exposed fireplaces and a warm and welcoming atmosphere. The inn is a free house and offers a wide choice of cask conditioned beers – many from private breweries. The range of food is also extensive and there is something to suit every taste. The menu changes from time to time and there are also 'special' dishes to choose from, with everything prepared on the premises. There is an attractive beer garden with benches. The inn is open on Monday to Saturday from 12 noon to 3 pm and 6.30 pm to 11 pm and on Sunday from 12 noon to 3 pm and 7 pm to 10.30 pm. Food is served from 12 noon to 2 pm and 6.30 pm to 9.30 pm (7 pm to 9.30 pm Sundays). Telephone: 01270 524223.

The Walk

① Leave the inn and pass through its front gate. Walk straight across the road, taking care, and go over a stile which is set in a fence on the opposite side. Keep to the left of a building and cross a large field, passing close to an isolated tree. Go over a stile at the far side of the field and cross the next field in the same direction as before. Cross two stiles in quick succession and follow a path which hugs the left hand edge of the next field. Go over a stile at the side of a gate and arrive at a crossing lane.

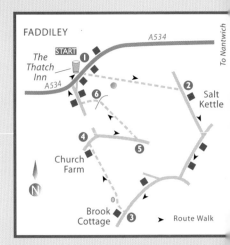

② Turn right along the lane. Pass dwelling called Salt Kettle and keep on arrive at a junction. Turn right here, enter Ikey Lane. Pass a dwelling calle Dodcot and on reaching the next junctic turn right in the direction of Larden Gree and Cholmondeley. After 80 yards fork le and pass a dwelling called Eastview. Kee along this attractive country lane for over mile to where, about 60 yards befo reaching a dwelling (Brook Cottage), the is a stile set in a hedgerow on the right.

③ Go over the stile and then, after yards, go over another stile in a crossi fence. Bear right now and converge with hedgerow on the right. Pass to the right a pond and then go over a stile on the rig Bear slightly left and cross two fields and over two stiles. Follow the next field ed and gradually move away from a hedger on your left. Arrive at a fence-stile which at the side of a gate close by Church Far an attractive house which is on the le Walk between an outbuilding and pond follow a gravel drive and then pass throu a gate to arrive at a crossing lane.

laneside cottage near Faddiley

) Turn right along the lane and after out 100 yards arrive at a junction. Turn ght here, in the direction of Swanley and cton. Keep on, past the delightful Ivy ottage, to where, about 250 yards further n, there is a footpath which begins rough a field gate on the left (50 yards fore Paddock Cottage is reached).

) Go through the gate and bear slightly ft to cross a large field to a stile which can : seen about 250 yards away. Go over the le and continue across the next field in e same general direction as before. Go er a stile at the field corner and after a rther 15 yards, cross a footbridge, which kes you over a stream.

) Care is required now, in order to follow e correct path. Having crossed the otbridge, you will see a dwelling about 0 yards away across a rough field. Aim to

the left of this dwelling and cross the field, passing close to a telegraph pole. Go over a stile in a facing hedgerow to arrive at a crossing lane. Turn right and arrive at a junction. Fork right and cross a road, taking care, and turn right to follow the roadside pavement. A few more strides take you back to the inn.

PLACES OF INTEREST NEARBY

About one mile from Nantwich, and reached via the A534 through Acton, is the magnificent **Dorfold Hall**. The hall is set amidst attractive gardens which are a delight during the summer months. The hall and gardens are usually open on Tuesdays and Bank Holiday Mondays – April to October, between 2 pm and 5 pm. Further east along the A534 is the fine old market town of **Nantwich**, famous for its half-timbered buildings and beautiful church.

Ravensmoor
The Farmers Arms

MAP: OS LANDRANGER 118 (GR 621505)   **WALK 28**   **DISTANCE:** 3¼ MILES

DIRECTIONS TO START: RAVENSMOOR IS 2 MILES TO THE SOUTH-WEST OF NANTWICH BETWEEN THE A530 AND A534. THE FARMERS ARMS IS IN THE CENTRE OF THE VILLAGE. **PARKING:** IN THE PUB CAR PARK, WITH PERMISSION. ALTERNATIVELY, THERE IS A SMALL PARKING LAYBY CLOSE TO THE HEAD OF SWANLEY LANE.

Ravensmoor is at the centre of a delightful tract of countryside to the south-west of the historic town of Nantwich. The Llangollen Branch of the Shropshire Union Canal cuts through this countryside on the western fringes of the village and this adds additional interest to the area. The walk initially follows an old lane away from the village before crossing a field path which leads to the canal towpath. A one mile stroll alongside the waterway is followed by a visit to the hamlet of Stoneley Green prior to returning to Ravensmoor along lanes and field paths.

The Farmers Arms

Situated on the old coaching route between Chester and London, The Farmers Arms is an extremely attractive country inn. Several hundred years old, the building has served as a smallholding, a shop, and a post office. Lagers, beers, cask ales, soft drinks and an extensive wine list make up the liquid refreshment on offer, whilst food, which is served every day between 12 noon and 2.30 pm and from 6.30 pm in the evening, is all prepared from fresh, locally grown produce. Bar snacks, lunches and four course meals can be purchased from a comprehensive and ever-changing menu. At the rear of the inn there is a large garden where trestle tables are set out on a lawned area interspersed with trees. There is also an attractive raised patio. Telephone: 01270 623522.

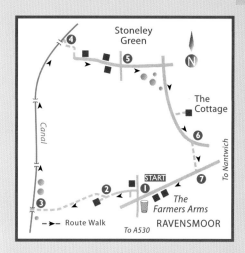

The Walk

1) On leaving the inn, cross the road and enter Swanley Lane in the direction of Swanley, Acton and Stoneley Green. After only 60 yards, and immediately on passing a telephone kiosk, turn left to enter Chapel Lane – which is headed by a no-through-road sign. Keep on, past Baddiley Close. Leave dwellings behind and follow a narrow lane. Pass the entrance drive of Fields Farm, where there is a crossing footpath. The lane becomes a gravel track and leads to a large gate set between stone pillars.

2) Go over a stile on the right here, to enter a large field. Turn left, and pass close to the corner hedge of a property, to go over a double stile and footbridge which are set in a crossing hedgerow. Cross the next field and go over a stile close to the junction of two hedgerows. Follow the next field edge, keeping a hedgerow on your immediate right. On reaching the end of the field go through a gate and then bear right to cross a large field. Arrive at a bridge. Do not cross this bridge but go to its right to join the towpath of the Shropshire Union Canal.

3) Turn right and follow the towpath away from the bridge (number 13). You are now walking alongside the Llangollen Branch of the canal which connects the Welsh town with the main course of the Shropshire Union Canal at Hurleston Junction. Follow the towpath for 1 mile and pass under three bridges. On passing under the third bridge, which is number 10, there is a fence-stile on the right.

4) Leave the towpath here and cross the fence-stile. Follow a grassy track away from the bridge. Go through a gate and turn right, to follow the edge of a field, keeping a hedgerow on your immediate right. On reaching the field corner, go through a gate

The Llangollen branch of the Shropshire Union Canal

and continue along a hedged-in track. The track leads to the head of a lane. Turn left and pass a picturesque thatched dwelling called End Cottage. Follow the lane past a number of other dwellings and after about ½ mile arrive at a crossing road.

⑤ Walk straight across the road, taking care, and enter a facing lane. A straight length of lane takes you to a junction of lanes. Do not enter the facing Dig Lane, but turn right here to enter Tally Ho Lane. Keep on past The Cottage, a dwelling which lies away from the lane on the left. About 250 yards further on, the lane turns to the left where a footpath sign points across a field on the right.

⑥ Go through a gate here, to enter a field. Turn left and cut across the field corner to go over a stile which is about 80 yards away.

Keep on across the next field, in the same general direction as before, and go over stile in a crossing hedgerow to arrive at crossing road.

⑦ Turn right and keep along the roadside A gentle stroll of just over ¼ mile takes yo back into Ravensmoor and the Farmer Arms.

PLACES OF INTEREST NEARBY

Less than 4 miles from Ravensmoor, and reache along the road which goes past the front door c the Farmers Arms, is the **Wrenbury Canal Sho** **at Wrenbury Mill**. The shop, which is adjacent t the lift bridge over the canal, sells quality ar gifts, and crafts related to canal life. The shop open 9 am to 6 pm Monday to Saturday an 10 am to 6 pm on Sundays. Telephone: 0127 780544.

Tushingham
The Blue Bell Inn

MAP: OS LANDRANGER 117 (GR 523454) **WALK 29** **DISTANCE:** 3 MILES

DIRECTIONS TO START: THE BLUE BELL INN IS SITUATED CLOSE BY THE A41 WHITCHURCH TO CHESTER ROAD AT BELL O' TH' HILL, WHICH IS ABOUT 3 MILES TO THE NORTH-WEST OF WHITCHURCH. **PARKING:** IN THE PUB CAR PARK, WITH PERMISSION.

Close to the Shropshire border, the scattered rural village of Tushingham is set amongst folds of lush green fields. This countryside has long been a favourite with those taking a break from the stresses of modern day life by hiring a boat on the Llangollen Branch of the Shropshire Union Canal – which cuts through the area on its way from Hurleston Junction into Wales. From the inn, the walk takes you along gently descending lanes, prior to joining a field path which leads to the towpath of the canal for a gentle mile alongside this delightful waterway. On leaving the canal towpath a field path takes you to a winding country lane for the stroll back to the Blue Bell Inn.

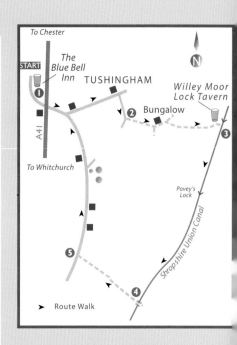

The Blue Bell Inn

For many years the inn was situated on the main road between Whitchurch and Chester, which in days gone by was a major coaching route. However, with the diversion of the A41 to a more easterly line, the inn now lies just off the main road in a much more peaceful setting. The origins of the inn go back many long years as is testified by that part of the building which was completed in 1667 being referred to as the 'new' part! Open every day, the inn provides a broad range of food and drink. There is a set menu with a choice of starters and options of main course include a 'large local trout'. Lasagne and various curries can be purchased as well as sandwiches and bowls of soup. There is also a special roast dinner provided every Sunday. Vegetarians are catered for but are requested to telephone ahead for specific daily menu details. Food is served every day between 12 noon and 3 pm and during the evening from 6 pm (7 pm on Sundays). Outside, there is a garden area with benches. Children (and animals) are made welcome. The inn is said to be haunted – by the ghost of a duck, whose spirit was bottled and then walled up somewhere in the building! Telephone: 01948 662172.

The Walk

① On leaving the inn turn left and follow the laneside pavement. Cross the main road, taking care, to enter a lane where a sign points toward Willey Moor. After only 60 yards turn left where the lane forks and gradually descend. On reaching the bottom of the descent turn right at a junction opposite a dwelling called Stockton's Bank. After a further 200 yards there is junction.

② Turn left to follow a track where a sign points to the Sandstone Trail. The track forks. Keep left here and pass a bungalow. After a further 50 yards go over a stile on the right to enter a field. Bear left and, on reaching the far side of the field, go over stile which is set between two large trees. Keep on across the next field and pass to the left of a telegraph pole. Cross a fence stile and then bear right to climb step which lead onto the towpath of the Shropshire Union Canal close by Willey Moor Lock Tavern.

③ Turn right and follow the canal towpath away from the Tavern. Walking alongside waterways is always enjoyable there is usually so much to see, whether be observing the wildlife – or the antics

Willey Moor Lock

the boatpeople. Pass Povey's Lock and then arrive at a bridge, which is number 26 (in total, you have strolled along the towpath for about 1 mile).

) Leave the towpath to the right of the bridge and pass over a stile to enter a large, undulating, field. Bear slightly right and gradually climb to the far corner of the field. (Note – on leaving the canalside a stile can be seen about 80 yards away over to the right – but ignore this and continue to the far corner of the field as directed.) Cross a stile at the field corner and then bear left across the next field. On reaching the far side of the field go over a stile at the side of a field gate to arrive at a crossing lane.

) Turn right along the lane and gradually climb. Pass Holly Bank and other dwellings. Ignore a turn off to the right and keep on past the imposing Georgian building of Tushingham House. There are long views ahead from this section of the lane towards the Peckforton Hills and beyond. Keep left at the next junction and arrive at a crossing road. Cross the road, taking care, to shortly arrive back at the Blue Bell Inn.

PLACES OF INTEREST NEARBY

The country town of **Malpas** is 3 miles by road to the north-west of Tushingham. The town has played an important role in the history of the county. The Romans had an encampment here and the Normans built a castle. Although only traces of these early settlements remain, the present-day town contains many interesting buildings and is dominated by a magnificent 14th century church.

Audlem
The Shroppie Fly

MAP: OS LANDRANGER 118 (GR 658436)   **WALK 30**   DISTANCE: 3 MILES

DIRECTIONS TO START: AUDLEM IS 6 MILES DUE SOUTH OF NANTWICH AT THE JUNCTION OF THE A525 AND A529. THE SHROPPIE FLY IS ON THE WEST SIDE OF THE TOWN BY THE SIDE OF THE SHROPSHIRE UNION CANAL. **PARKING:** IN THE PUB CAR PARK, WITH PERMISSION. ALTERNATIVELY, THERE IS A PUBLIC CAR PARK CLOSE TO THE TOWN CENTRE.

Audlem, which is at the centre of a thriving farming area, is Cheshire's most southerly town. The Shropshire Union Canal, linking Shropshire to the Cheshire Plain, passes through a series of 15 locks on the western fringes of the town. The canal drops some 93 feet over a distance of 1¼ miles through these locks. In its prime the cargoes included coal, fuel oils and iron ore which fed all the industries along the canal t Liverpool. From the canalside, the walk take you through the town centre where there is a opportunity to visit the magnificent mediev: church of St James, prior to following min lanes past well-kept cottages. A mixture of fie paths, tracks and lanes then lead through som lush green countryside on the circular rou back to the town.

The Shroppie Fly

Opposite the 13th lock in the series of 15, the Shroppie Fly's origins go back as far as the construction of the canal, for the building was originally a canalside warehouse which was in use up to 1970. Following an extensive conversion, the pub was opened for business during 1974. Its unusual name relates to the fact that the bar is partly constructed from a vessel called *The Shroppie Fly*. The 'fly' boats were fast, passenger-carrying vessels, which operated day and night. Apart from the unique bar, there is a large exposed fireplace and shelves full of interesting books. The pub is a freehouse, hence there is a wide variety of liquid refreshment on offer. Food is available every day from 12 noon to 2.30 pm and 6 pm to 9 pm. There is a range of starters, main dishes, vegetarian dishes, side orders, ploughman's lunches and jacket potatoes. Children have their own menu and various sandwiches can be purchased. There is usually a specials board in operation as well as a tempting selection of sweets. When the weather is fine there are outside tables and benches from where all the canal activity can be observed. Telephone: 01270 811772.

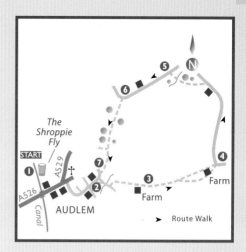

e Walk

) On leaving the inn turn left and follow e canalside road past Audlem Mill Canal op and Workshop. Pass the Bridge Inn d then turn left to stroll into the centre of e town. Turn right by the church to enter afford Street. The way is immediately ht now, to enter a lane opposite the urch steps but first of all, if time allows, e a look in and around the church.

The origins of the church go back to the 13th century and it contains many items of interest. There is some excellent stained-glass and the lofty nave roof has been restored to good effect.

Enter the lane which begins opposite the church steps and immediately pass The Old Priest-House. Descend, and follow the lane as it turns to the left. On the left now there is a nursing home, which was once a grammar school dating from 1655. Keep on past Daisy Cottage and bear right to arrive at a crossing road.

② Cross the road and enter a facing lane. After only 50 yards bear right to follow a narrow hedged-in lane. At the next junction turn right where a sign on a wall says 'Salford'. Cross a bridge and then, 80 yards further on, leave the lane to the left, to follow a narrow footpath which goes past Lower Beck Cottage. Cross a stile and enter a field. Follow a well-defined path which gradually bears to the right. Go over a stile at the field corner and then pass to the left of a hedge which juts out into the field to gradually climb up a field edge, keeping a fence on your immediate right.

There is a farm over to the right here. Bear left near the end of the field and then go over a stile at the side of a gate.

③ Follow a track between fences. After about 500 yards pass through a gate which is about 300 yards before the track reaches a farm. Go over a stile on the right here, to enter a large field. Turn left and gradually bear right to walk away from the track which is on your left side. Go over a stile in a crossing fence and then pass to the right of farm outbuildings. The path hugs a fence on the left and takes you past a tennis court. Go over a stile at the side of a gate and turn right to arrive at a bend in a crossing lane.

④ Turn left along the lane and immediately pass a large dwelling called The Highlands. The lane gradually descends and goes past Bank House. Turn next left here to enter a hedged-in track. Pass a dwelling and arrive at a gate in front of a house called Willow Farm. Turn left here and go over a stile which gives access to a narrow path which follows the edge of the property. Pass over two stiles in quick succession. Bear right now, and cross a rough field, to go over a footbridge which takes you over a stream. Climb up a facing field and gradually bear left to converge with a hedgerow on the left. On reaching the field corner go over a stile to arrive at a crossing lane.

⑤ Turn left along the lane. Keep on past Hope Cottage and Ivy House to where, 50 yards further on, the lane turns sharply to the right at a facing dwelling.

⑥ Leave the lane to the left here, to follow a path which skirts around the dwelling. Follow a well-defined hedged-in path for about ¼ mile and emerge at a bend in a track. Keep forward here, in the direction of a house which can be seen about 200 yards away. Follow the track past the house, and other dwellings, and arrive at a crossing road.

⑦ Turn left and keep on past minor lanes which go off to the left, to arrive at a crossing road. Cross the road and enter School Lane. You are now back on part of your initial route. Bear left past Daisy Cottage and follow the facing lane back into the town centre to turn left again for the short stroll back to the Shroppie Fly.

PLACES OF INTEREST NEARBY

Between Nantwich and Audlem, and generally running parallel with the A529, there is a secondary road which connects the A530 near Nantwich with the A525 near Audlem. Directions at both ends of this lane lead to one of Cheshire's more unusual attractions – **a secret bunker**. The site, at Hack Green, was to have been Cheshire's headquarters in the event of a nuclear war. There are radio rooms, a BBC studio, a decontamination room, two cinemas, a radar museum, communications centre, military vehicles and canteen and shop. The bunker is open from 1st March to 31st October between 10 am and 5 pm every day and also every weekend throughout the winter season and all bank holidays (except Christmas Day and Boxing Day). Telephone 01270 629219.